# REMBRANDT

Otto Benesch

SKIRA

*RIZZOLI*
NEW YORK

First published 1957
First paperback edition 1990

Published in the United States of America in 1990 by

𝑅IZZOLI INTERNATIONAL PUBLICATIONS, INC.
300 Park Avenue South, New York 10010

© 1990 by Editions d'Art Albert Skira S.A., Geneva

Library of Congress Catalog Card Number 89-43607
ISBN 0-8478-1216-2

Printed in Switzerland

# CONTENTS

# REMBRANDT'S LIFE

FOR an artist of the seventeenth century, when the journey to Italy was regarded as an obligatory finishing touch to his training and painters, sculptors and architects traveled extensively in Europe on artistic, commercial and even diplomatic missions, Rembrandt's life was outwardly uneventful. He never once crossed the narrow frontiers of his native land—his alleged visit to England is a legend—and from beginning to end his destiny as an artist worked itself out in Holland alone.

In Rembrandt's time Holland enjoyed a position of worldwide importance in the community of nations; as a haven both for intellectual endeavor and for business enterprise, it attracted the vital forces of the age and opened a gateway on the outside world. That Rembrandt never used that gateway as a means of access to court circles is characteristic of this great artist. His mind was a world in itself, rich with the experience of his inner life. He had no need to travel; a painting or drawing, even a mere print coming casually to hand, was enough to conjure up before his inner vision all the grandeur and majesty of Italian art. In the same way he was familiar with the best period of German art, the age of Schongauer, Dürer and Holbein, with the world of the Persian miniature painters and Indian Mogul princes, with the Jewish and Islamic East, even with ancient Rome and Greece. A piece of cloth, a utensil or a piece of sculpture, a sword or helmet, was enough for this great visionary to weave his spell and bring vanished worlds to life again. Such were Rembrandt's travels, these were the realms in which his spirit ranged. With him the inner life was everything.

Also his private life was richer in dramatic human experience than that of most of his contemporaries. Though confined to the narrow bounds of two Dutch cities, his career spanned the full circle from wealth and prosperity—"*ex superabundanti*" was how he described his former affluence before the court of justice—to direst poverty; from domestic happiness and security in early days to loneliness and isolation in old age, from brief celebrity to oblivion once his work had gone out of fashion.

Rembrandt Harmensz. van Rijn was born into a lower middle-class family on July 15, 1606, in the old university town of Leiden. His father, Harmen Gerritsz., was a miller, well-to-do in a modest way. The family took its name from the Rhine, on one arm of which his father's mill stood. It was in a house in the Weddesteeg, a lane on the rampart of Leiden overlooking the river, that Rembrandt was born. His mother, Neeltje Willemsdochter van Zuytbrouck, was a pious soul whom we often see in Rembrandt's pictures, perusing the Bible or figuring in a biblical scene with the stately dignity of a prophetess or a sibyl. She it was no doubt who gave him his lifelong predilection for the Book of Books.

Rembrandt's six brothers and sisters grew up beside him. After the older boys had adopted various trades, Gerrit becoming a miller, Willem a baker and Adriaen a cobbler, his father decided to train Rembrandt for a learned profession. The youngest child of the family was Lijsbeth, who is also familiar to us from her brother's paintings. Presumably she kept house for him during the early years in Amsterdam, for in the pictures of that period the features of his attractive sister gradually merge into those of Saskia. Even as a child Rembrandt must have shown signs of an exceptional intelligence, for his father's decision to send him to the local Latin School proves that he was considered capable of qualifying for the relatively high position of a jurist or divine. After completing the seven-year course of classical studies, which certainly contributed not a little to establishing his status in later years as a "learned painter," he was enrolled as a student at Leiden University on May 20, 1620.

But the lure of art was evidently too strong; for he soon cut short his classical studies and entered the workshop of a local painter, Jacob Isaaksz. van Swanenburch, under whom he studied as an apprentice for three years. What we know of this teacher from his few extant works makes it highly improbable that Rembrandt acquired anything more from him than the technical foundations of drawing and painting. Possibly it was through Swanenburch that he came in contact with the engraving of Jacques Callot; on the other hand, the sheer abundance of this master draftsman's output had made his work so familiar to the art circles of every country in Europe that this contact might easily have been made elsewhere.

After leaving Swanenburch's studio, Rembrandt also felt the need to leave Leiden, in search of wider horizons. He accordingly moved to Amsterdam where he studied for six months with Pieter Lastman, whose teaching gave his art what was to be its distinctive imprint. According to Houbraken, he also worked for a time under Jacob Pynas, an Amsterdam painter stylistically akin to Lastman.

Though of much shorter duration than his Leiden apprenticeship, this period of study in Amsterdam had a sudden and decisive effect on the shaping of Rembrandt's artistic personality. After his return to Leiden he started work as an independent artist; his earliest known works—drawings and paintings—date from about 1625. He and a fellow student, Jan Lievens, slightly younger than himself, fitted up a studio together and the two friends, inspired by the same ideals, eagerly set to work in close collaboration. In his autobiography the Dutch poet and humanist Constantijn Huygens has left a vivid account of a visit to the studio of Lievens and Rembrandt, whose wholehearted devotion to their craft impressed him greatly. In addition to his creative genius Rembrandt possessed a strong natural bent for teaching which even in this youthful period attracted several pupils to him—but the material benefit they brought him can only have been slight. Gerard Dou and Jan Joris van Vliet were his most significant Leiden pupils.

He and his friend painted, etched and drew untiringly, often long after dark in winter so as to make good use of the long northern nights. He worked from the living model: poor folk fetched in from the streets or old folk from the poor-house, more often members of his own family, and even his own face. Since it was his family whose members also posed for Lievens, very probably the Leiden studio was located in one of the outbuildings attached to the family house of the Van Rijns, who were fairly prosperous, whereas Lievens' father was a poor silk embroiderer.

As the narrative in Huygens' autobiography makes clear, Rembrandt early attracted the attention of Dutch connoisseurs and the strange young man, such as we see him in the Boston self-portrait beside a huge easel, must have been regarded as something of a prodigy. Arent van Buchel wrote at the time: "There is much to do about a Leiden miller's son, but rather prematurely." The Dutch of that period delighted in seeing themselves and their surroundings represented in paintings. So that the interest aroused by young Rembrandt soon led to his receiving portrait commissions from well-to-do burghers, first in his native town, then in Amsterdam.

The untiring investigator of reality, given to brooding over the Bible and accustomed to going his own way, now had to comply with the wishes of his sitters and even gradually acquire the polish of a man of the world. The wealthy merchant Nicolaes Ruts, the courtier Huygens and the famous anatomy professor Dr Tulp would never have come to him with their portrait commissions, had he been likely to

*An Artist in his Studio, 1632. Private Collection, Great Britain.*

transpose them into a world of fantasy as he did his parents and his brothers and sisters, or to analyse and caricature them as he did his own face. They expected him to abide by the well-established conventions of portraiture—which the ambitious youth did, but not without extracting from them new and startling effects and outclassing famous colleagues in their own special field. But no serious competition could be looked for in Leiden, whose school of painters was by that time of merely local importance; only in cosmopolitan Amsterdam could he give his full measure.

Commissioned in 1632 to paint a life-size group portrait of Professor Tulp's anatomy class, he took the opportunity to move to Amsterdam for good, as obviously he stood a better chance of getting further commissions of this kind as a resident of the metropolis than as an intermittent visitor. Economic considerations may have been the chief inducement, but once in his new surroundings he found fresh and stimulating sources of inspiration.

Rembrandt took lodgings with the painter and art dealer Hendrick van Uylenburch, whose house stood on the corner of the Zwanenburgwal and the Anthonies-Breestraat (now Jodenbreestraat). In this he may have been prompted not only by his personal acquaintanceship with Uylenburch, but also by the fact that the house was located at the entrance of the Amsterdam ghetto with its old houses and venerable synagogues—a place where the colorful world of the Old Testament was still a living presence. Rembrandt always relied on the firsthand experience of real life to fire his creative imagination.

In Uylenburch's home he met his host's cousin, an orphan girl named Saskia, who came of a notable patrician family of Leeuwarden, in Friesland, and whose father had been the local burgomaster. The young people were attracted to each other and their betrothal took place on July 5, 1633; to celebrate the occasion Rembrandt made a charming silverpoint portrait of Saskia (Kupferstichkabinett, Berlin). They were married a year later, on July 10, 1634, in the small parish church of St Anne at Het Bilt.

Rembrandt's marriage with Saskia was an extremely happy one. His success as an artist combined with Saskia's affluence and social standing soon led to Rembrandt's rise in the social scale, a circumstance that spared him the material worries that have crippled the efforts of so many artists, and filled him with an overbrimming sense of power and freedom.

His paintings of the 1630s, in their exuberant fantasy, vouch for this. He shrank from no difficulty and vied not only with the best painters of Holland, but with the leading Baroque painters of Catholic Europe. He filled numerous portrait commissions, produced a wealth of black-and-white work, and gathered many pupils around him. Among them, during that first decade in Amsterdam, we find such names as Backer, Bol, Flinck, Victors, Philips Koninck and Van den Eeckhout. Though Rembrandt carried out a certain amount of graphic work in collaboration with his pupils, following the practice obtaining in Rubens' studio, as a rule he allowed them far more freedom than the Flemish master had done, and sought rather to bring out the individuality of each pupil, who was expected to make his way toward Rembrandt by drawing on his own resources.

These teaching methods are to be accounted for partly by the type of art produced in Holland, where with rare exceptions the large-scale official commissions current in Catholic countries were unknown; partly, too, by Rembrandt's personal temperament, his attitude to his art and his fellow men. While in his youth he inscribed the following couplet in the album of a German traveler:

An upright mind
Holds honor above estate,

what in latter years he valued most in his relations with others was "not so much honor as freedom" (Houbraken). Individual freedom seemed to this great teacher more important than all the drilling of the schools. How close in many cases the pupils came to the master, out of inner compulsion and veneration for him, is shown by the difficult problems of critical attribution raised by the Rembrandt œuvre, particularly by the paintings.

As the activities of a busy studio would have sorely taxed the accommodation of a private home, Rembrandt fitted up for his use one of the fine old warehouses that can still be seen today on the canal banks in the heart of Amsterdam, and it was there, very probably, that he painted such large-scale works as the *Night Watch* and the *Julius Civilis*. It was only later, when he bought a spacious house in the Breestraat, that he had a "schilderkamer" of his own and plenty of room for his pupils, amongst whom he spent many pleasant hours sketching from the life.

Encouraged by his new prosperity, Rembrandt's taste for collecting developed into a passion that later contributed to his financial difficulties. He collected not only the choice garments and jewelry in which he decked his young wife when she posed for him, not only the curios, precious objects and old weapons which he needed as a painter, but also paintings, drawings, prints, miniatures and sculptures which together probably made up the most universal and many-sided collection of his time. All the great names of painting, from Jan van Eyck to Rubens and Seghers, were represented in it. Rembrandt became a familiar figure in the Amsterdam auction halls and his expert judgments carried weight. Possibly in the beginning (as was not unusual in Holland) a commercial motive entered into this activity, for we find Rembrandt describing himself in a notarized power of attorney as a "coopman," i.e. a dealer.

It would be a mistake, however, to reproach him on this account with being materialistic or mercenary, in the same way as Titian— perhaps on better grounds—has been reproached with his peasant-like solicitude for the material well-being of his family. What Rembrandt earned with his pictures he spent so freely and lavishly on collecting works of art that his contemporaries regarded him as an eccentric spendthrift; yet no one was more temperate in his personal needs than he. His completely irrational standards of valuation (according to

Baldinucci) both as regards his own productions and those of others prove that, in his eyes, the value of a work of art transcended the bounds of the materially measurable.

The real cause of his financial downfall was the purchase in 1639 of a mansion in the Breestraat, next door to Uylenburch's property, which committed him to the payment of heavy installments over a period of years.

Today that house is a venerated memorial giving us an intimate picture of the surroundings in which he lived and worked from day to day. There Rembrandt experienced not only the inspired throes of artistic creation and the joys of a happy married life, but also the grief of personal bereavement. Neither his first child Rumbartus nor the two little daughters who followed successively, both christened Cornelia, lived more than a few months. As for Saskia, whose luminous, transparent beauty we admire in so many of the artist's finest works, soon her health gave way. Her touching features are immortalized in many drawings showing her bedridden, either ailing or recovering from childbirth.

Rembrandt sought and found relief from his domestic worries not only in his work, but in the company of fellow artists and a circle of learned friends that included both Christian theologians, such as Sylvius, Uytenbogaert and Anslo, and the great rabbi Menasseh ben Israel and the physician Ephraim Bueno, neighbors of his in the Jewish quarter of Amsterdam. Of his best friends he etched and painted eloquent portraits. Rembrandt's connection with the Jewish world was, in virtue of his whole spiritual outlook on men and things, a very deep and intimate one. He himself, according to an old account, belonged not to the national Reformed Church, strictly Calvinistic, but to the Mennonite sect, whose origins go back to the Anabaptist movement of the early sixteenth century and to the kindred religious group of the Moravian Brethren.

While busily engaged at the beginning of the 1640s on the *Night Watch* and other major works, Rembrandt suffered the tragic loss of those nearest and dearest to him. First his mother died, in September 1640, she whom he revered and had so often portrayed. A ray of light came with the birth of his son Titus, baptized on September 22, 1641. This was the only one of his children to live, and the great monumental painting of *Manoah's Sacrifice* in the Dresden Gallery, in which the angel announces the birth of a son to Gideon's parents, rings like a hymn of thanksgiving on Rembrandt's part for the long-desired arrival of a male heir.

But the young mother, her health broken, survived the event only a few months. As Rembrandt wrestled with the mighty task of the *Night Watch*, Saskia wrestled with death; on June 14, 1642, she died, aged barely thirty.

This must have come as a terrible shock to Rembrandt, for in the light of his art we can guess what Saskia meant to him, kindling and inspiring his imagination in all his work. She lives for us in many a canvas, whether biblical (Delilah), mythological (Flora and Danaë), or simply and happily mundane (the Dresden double portrait). Then abruptly, after the abounding joy, the radiant delights of his life with Saskia, came darkness.

We may well imagine the sudden introversion of the man who a few years before had gloried in his triumphant successes and boundless powers, the man who had delighted in portraying himself as the biblical hero Samson. While Saskia lay dying, her features haunted his fervid imagination and pursued him into the thick of the soldiery peopling the *Night Watch*, conjuring up a world of strange imaginings in which we see her in the guise of a child, in a realm of fantasy where Time has ceased to be. And after she had departed from this world, he painted her again from memory in the great Berlin portrait of 1643, an all-glorious epitaph.

This revaluation of all life's values can have been no easy task for the artist, who now entered on a trying period of readjustment. He had to find himself anew, and had to do so under the pressure of a middle-class society whose religious, social and economic laws were

*Rembrandt and his Wife Saskia, 1636.*
*Rijksmuseum, Amsterdam.*

inflexible, and which had hitherto followed his career with mixed feelings of admiring recognition and vague resentment. Rembrandt's subsequent evolution can only be described as a step-by-step process of inner and outer liberation. The world's opinion of him mattered less to him now. While in the past he had given society what it expected of him, and in fact to its amazement had given it far more than its expectations, he turned now into ways of his own.

The conflict began already with the *Night Watch*, in which he overstepped an old-established convention that even Frans Hals had never transgressed but had only revitalized in his incomparable way. Rembrandt proceeded to reinterpret the traditional Dutch corporation portrait as a human drama withdrawn from the here-and-now and transmuted, like Shakespeare's tragedies, into a lofty poetic unity transcending actuality.

Opposition must have been brewing even then and only kept from bursting into the open by the personal prestige of Frans Banning Cocq, the Civic Guard officer who commissioned the work. With this bold performance began Rembrandt's emancipation from the ambitions which he had pursued in the previous decade, and which now meant nothing to him.

The 1640s were at first a period of groping and experiment, as we see most noticeably in the drawings. As Rembrandt broke free of the conventions of the "modern art" of his day (i.e. international Baroque), he had to build for himself a new world of forms—a difficult undertaking for any artist, and one in which he can hardly count on the understanding of contemporaries. What others thought of his efforts was by now, however, a matter of indifference to him, and his withdrawal from the world in its initial stages can only be regarded as a voluntary one, the more so as he had already become a celebrity.

He became particular in his choice of the commissions he accepted and there was a decline in the number of portraits he produced of people outside his own circle. Likenesses of friends and relatives now represent his best work in portraiture: in-laws from Saskia's family, fellow artists, his frame-maker, clerical and humanist friends, outstanding among them young Jan Six, scion of one of the leading patrician families of Amsterdam. Oftener than in the past an initial portrait study in the form of a drawing or an oil was followed up by an etching. His activities as an etcher increasingly absorbed him and resulted—often after years of work on the plates—in prints whose velvety depths and magic play of light match those of his paintings. Now that they went entirely to works of his own choosing, his energies knew no bounds. He was untroubled by further orders for corporation portraits, no guild or Civic Guard group being prepared to run the risk of a second *Night Watch*.

The joy had gone out of his domestic life with Saskia's death. He engaged a trumpeter's widow, Geertghe Dircx, to look after little Titus and keep house for him. The relations of the lonely artist with Geertghe, whom he portrayed and regaled with trinkets and jewelry, later had a deplorable conclusion: a suit for breach of promise. An hysteric, she finally was interned in an insane asylum at Gouda. Since it was Rembrandt's practice all his life to sketch and paint those nearest him, we may be sure that *her* portrait too figures, unrecognized, somewhere in his work (perhaps she posed for the *Bathsheba* of 1643, in the Metropolitan Museum, New York).

About 1645 there entered his house the gentle soul who was to grace the remaining years of his life: Hendrickje Stoffels Jegers. She came of a family of soldiers living at Bredevoort, a small town on the German frontier. From now on, after he had first recorded her very likeable features in the Dulwich College portrait, she sat again and again for various figures in Rembrandt's biblical compositions.

In the years following Saskia's death he often fled the loneliness and, sometimes, the dissensions that filled his house. He sought the freedom of the open air and in the course of long rambles through Amsterdam and its environs covered the pages of his sketchbooks with landscape drawings; on the basis of these Frits Lugt was able to re-constitute Rembrandt's itineraries in an unusually interesting book (*Mit Rembrandt in Amsterdam*, Berlin 1920). He is also known to have made short trips to old towns in the neighboring provinces. For the peace and happiness that had fled his home he may have found some compensation in his friendship with other artists and intellectuals, such as Jan Six and the painters Cappelle, Sorgh and Asselijn. His work with his pupils too, among whom we find so great a painter as Carel Fabritius, must have been a source of pleasure to him.

From the outward show of drama and emotion that had meant so much to him in his youth, he turned increasingly to the silent dramas enacted in the secret places of the heart. Schmidt-Degener rightly pointed to what he called a "Holy Year" in Rembrandt's life: the year in which he painted the Louvre *Supper at Emmaus* and presumably finished the *Hundred Guilder Print*. His art had turned inward. The long procession of meditative figures, passing before us in his paintings, tells us little now of the surroundings in which the artist moved, but much about his inner life. The few portraits he still made to order differ hardly at all from the many portraits he painted on his own initiative, figures which, though simple and straightforward, issue from a wonder-world of poetry in a far deeper sense than do the ostentatious, fancifully draped figures of his early period. Rembrandt had achieved that inner and outer freedom which he himself had declared to be the only worthwhile aim in life. He had built up a world of his own in which he ranged at will, and this private realm appears in retrospect as a whole art epoch in its own right at a time—the decade from about 1650 to 1660 was the classical apogee of Dutch painting—when his aims and those of his contemporaries briefly coincided before finally separating for good. In his own world he stood on an equal footing with the other great ages of painting and their standard-bearers who belong now more and more to the past.

For Rembrandt was, as Schmidt-Degener aptly expressed it, "the last of the Renaissance artists." Though he declined to make the journey to Italy, at that time almost a professional obligation for every Northern artist, he was always a sincere admirer of Italian and ancient art; and though he no longer emulated his great predecessors, as he had in his youth, he discovered, independently, similar and no less valid solutions of the eternal problems of art.

Peace and harmony had again descended on his home thanks to Hendrickje, who in her shy, devoted way soon became a second wife to him. Although their union never received the sanction of the church (a clause in Saskia's will stipulating that should he remarry he forfeited the usufruct accruing from her estate), she remained at his side, a faithful helpmate and a devoted stepmother to Titus, despite the gossip of their fellow citizens and the admonitions of the puritanical church council. In 1655 she bore him a daughter whom he named Cornelia in memory of Saskia's two little daughters who both had died in infancy. The features of Hendrickje and young Titus, now growing up, are familiar to us from the many pictures in which they appear. The boy studied painting under his father, but later gave it up to become an art dealer.

In the long run no artist can set himself up with impunity against the conventions of a community founded on a firm social and economic basis—and this was impossible even in the free Holland of the seventeenth century. With Saskia no longer there to look after it, Rembrandt's fortune rapidly melted away. While his collections continued to grow, his income steadily diminished as he took to working more for himself and less for others. Although his fame had spread all over Europe, and though such influential friends as Jan Six still procured important commissions for him (notably for a historical panel to figure over the fireplace in the new City Hall, and the second *Anatomy Lesson*), the financial ruin threatening him could not be averted.

Rembrandt was in arrears with the payments due on his large house in the Breestraat of Amsterdam. He stood on friendly terms with the previous owner, Christoffel Thijssens, whose country house at Saxenburg he had painted (with Thijssens hunting in the foreground) and etched (the so-called *Gold-Weigher's Field*), but this failed to check the peremptory summonses served on him for payments overdue. To meet these Rembrandt entered into further financial commitments. By the mid-fifties we find him staggering under a load of fresh debts incurred to meet the old ones.

Finally there was no way out and in July 1656 the artist appealed to the City Council of Amsterdam for a *cessio bonorum*, i.e. the formal surrender of his goods and chattels to his creditors; this, at the time, was the most honorable means of declaring bankruptcy, securing the debtor from degradation and leaving him with the bare necessities of life. A *cessio bonorum* was forthwith granted him on the formal grounds of "business reverses and losses at sea," and the insolvency chamber began the liquidation of his property, an inventory of which was filed on July 25, 1656.

This document is one of our most important sources of information regarding Rembrandt's artistic personality. As against a surprising paucity of household goods and everything contributing to the comfort of the home, we find a list of works of art that reads like the catalogue of an extensive museum: besides picture and print collections, a collection of antiques including both originals and plaster casts. In the following years three auctions took place: one of his art collection, another of his house and its appurtenances, and a third of his collection of drawings and sketches, including the large series of Rembrandt's own drawings classified by their subjects in separate portfolios.

The prices fetched, as is always the case at forced sales, represented a mere fraction of their value. Rembrandt's creditors recovered only a part of their dues and he would have found himself compelled to surrender the whole of his subsequent production to them had not Titus and Hendrickje saved the situation by taking a step that was perfectly lawful. This was the creation in 1658 of a firm dealing in works of art under their management. Two years later Rembrandt became their employee under an agreement which, in return for his entire production, furnished him with wages, food and lodging. Thus the artist was left in peace to carry on his work untroubled by the machinations of speculators. He moved to a modest lodging in the Rozengracht on the west side of the city.

In spite of the harassing events that preyed on Rembrandt's time and peace of mind during these years, they were by far the most artistically fruitful and significant period of his whole career. No untoward event could stifle for long his creative ardor. The triumph of his indomitable spirit over reverses and hardship is allegorized in the *Phoenix* etching. It is almost as if his struggle against heavy odds spurred him on to his greatest achievement in the field of monumental painting, the *Conspiracy of Julius Civilis* which, perhaps through his old friend

Jan Six, he was commissioned in 1661 to paint for Amsterdam's new City Hall.

Man himself—this was the subject and substance of the art of his old age. An arresting autobiography unfolds itself before us in his painted self-portraits, as numerous now as the etched self-portraits of his youth. The wisdom and profound understanding born of a life's experience may have made the old master a less egocentric, more objective judge of his fellow men; in any event, there came a surprising increase in the number of portrait commissions he received and accepted, all carried out with so deep a spiritual insight that they seem like subjects of his own choosing. It is a tribute to the judgment of his fellow citizens, the wardens of the Drapers' Guild, that they now gave him the opportunity of producing his greatest work in the field of the group portrait.

At the beginning of the 1660s Rembrandt seems to have stood at the summit of his powers. Now that he was on the threshold of old age, the loss of the faithful few on whom he could still depend must have been all the harder to bear. On July 24, 1663, he saw Hendrickje to her grave. Living more in his private world than in the world of reality and with no one to befriend him he soon became the prey once more of speculators, ever ready to exploit his unquenchable passion for collecting.

As soon as he came of age, however, Titus took many of the burdens off his father's shoulders. Abroad Rembrandt enjoyed an international reputation, but in his own country, living as he did in voluntary obscurity, he soon became a forgotten man. The number of his pupils dwindled; among them was that sensitive artist Aert de Gelder. His last support fell away when early in 1668 Titus died after one year of marriage, leaving behind him a young widow and child. This was a shock from which Rembrandt never recovered. However much the conditions of his life were those of his own choosing, the fact remains that his last years were clouded by the most galling, wholly undeserved poverty and that none of his friends came to his aid. Shortly

gereken: door Rembrant van Rhyn naer Syn selver
soo als hy in syn Schilder kamer gekleet was.

*Rembrandt Standing, in his Painter's Smock, 1655. Rembrandt House, Amsterdam.*

before his death he complained to his housekeeper that he had to draw on the savings of his daughter Cornelia in order to cover his household expenses.

He died on October 4, 1669, aged sixty-three, after a life poor in outward events but vastly rich in inner experiences. The laconic inscription in the death register of the Westerkerk runs as follows: "The 8th of October, 1669, Rembrandt van Rijn, painter, domiciled in the Rozengracht opposite the Doolhof, bier with 16 bearers, leaves behind two children . . . Fee 20 guilders."

*Tobit and Anna, 1626. Rijksmuseum, Amsterdam.*

# MICROCOSM

## THE LEIDEN YEARS

O F ALL Rembrandt's work it was the paintings that were least appreciated by his contemporaries. Although unknown outside a small circle of initiates, the drawings were held by them in the highest esteem, while the etchings, warmly praised and sought after even in his lifetime, earned him an international reputation. The paintings, however, particularly those of his later years, were continually meeting with critical reservations or objections, the early ones being considered too bold, too impetuous, and the later ones "outmoded." In some verses he wrote as a warning to Philips Koninck, the Dutch poet Vondel compared Rembrandt—though without mentioning his name—to an owl dwelling in the shadows and called him "a son of darkness." His chiaroscuro ran counter to the contemporary vogue for brightly colored paintings. The whole style of his paintings was a stumbling-block even to such eminent judges of a later day as William Blake and Jakob Burckhardt, and academic-minded critics did not fail to point out his defects, even when they themselves owed him a large but of course unacknowledged debt (such was the case with Sir Joshua Reynolds).

Yet it is precisely Rembrandt's painting which, from the nineteenth century on, has won him the unique place he now occupies in the history of art and has exerted a revolutionary influence. Today in the minds of millions of people Rembrandt is the Prince of Painters and is known to them only by the work of his brush.

There are many strands in Rembrandt's art linking it up with that of his predecessors and contemporaries. He sprang from an art current which, by the time he came on the scene, no longer held so dominant a position as in the preceding decades, and which appealed above all to the educated classes, to connoisseurs, to those who had been to Italy and were familiar with the classical poets. Rembrandt's teacher Pieter Lastman belonged to that group of Dutch artists who, like Rubens, had traveled to Rome in the first decade of the new century and come under the influence of the great German painter Adam Elsheimer, a master of light and landscape. Among them, in addition to Lastman, we find Jan and Jacob Pynas and Nicolaes Moeyaert. They shared Elsheimer's admiration for Caravaggio's realism and owed the basic elements of their style to him. Rembrandt may therefore be described as an indirect pupil of Elsheimer. He never met this great teacher, who died in 1610, long before he embarked on his career as an artist, but he knew his pictures well for having collected them assiduously and he continued to draw inspiration from them even late in life.

So it came about that, though he never made the journey to Italy, Rembrandt was nourished on the art of those who had done so, the so-called Italianists, whose erudite style still, generally speaking, dominated Dutch painting at the end of the sixteenth century, but was now losing ground before the rising tide of native Dutch naturalism. The group of Caravaggio's and Elsheimer's followers in Amsterdam had for its counterpart a similar group in Catholic Utrecht: Honthorst, Terbrugghen, Baburen, and the engraver Goudt, who had also been to Italy and were admirers of Caravaggesque realism. Rembrandt was well acquainted with the work of these artists and to them too he certainly owed much.

Like their German model, the Amsterdam Caravaggeschi of the Elsheimer persuasion favored small-sized paintings and produced works for private collectors. The Utrecht group, on the other hand, often supplied devotional pictures to Catholic churches and were accustomed to the large formats in vogue in Italy. Lastman, like Elsheimer, preferred wooden panels or copper plates as a support for the colors, alternately earthy or luminous, that he used in his biblical and mythological scenes, saturating them with atmosphere and rhetorically stressing the expressive play of features to the point of theatricality. Here there was much for Rembrandt to learn: composition and figure grouping, facial expression and dramatic gesture, and, finally, the use of color as a means of conveying atmosphere. Although he spent only six months with Lastman, he made the most of what he learned from him and by about 1624 could establish himself as a master on his own account.

Rembrandt's earliest known works go back to about 1624-1625. These consist of several drawings and one painting, an *Adoration of the Magi*. This small panel is still the work of a raw youth, though its awkward, ponderous, unmastered figures contain intimations of the grandeur and fullness of his later forms. The scene is bathed in cool, bluish moonlight, with the Star of Bethlehem shining out amid a host of lesser lights, as in Elsheimer's small nightpieces. This is but a prelude; the full orchestra sets in only in 1626, and from then on a steady succession of signed and dated works enables us to follow the artist's evolution year by year.

The research work of the past few decades has resulted in a sharp increase in the number of paintings assigned to the Leiden period, and these now provide us with an accurate picture of Rembrandt's youthful activity. They confirm Huygens' shrewd observation to the effect that young Rembrandt aimed at concentrating his vast pictorial conceptions in small-sized pictures, thereby continuing the tradition deriving from Elsheimer and handed on to him by Lastman. Although by 1626 he had ventured on biblical and historical compositions containing

*The Stoning of St Stephen, 1625. Musée des Beaux-Arts, Lyon.*

several figures (*Balaam's Ass*, Musée Cognacq-Jay, Paris, and the *Justice of Brutus*, Lakenhal, Leiden), the most successful of his early paintings are those with few figures, for example *Tobit and Anna* (Rijksmuseum, Amsterdam), monumental despite its small dimensions. Here, although diminutive, figures take on something of the majestic proportions of the Old Testament patriarchs in the Sistine Chapel. The style of the work is that of Caravaggesque realism. With passionate fidelity the young painter recorded the wrinkles of wizened faces and the tattered patchwork of what once perhaps had been splendid raiment but now gave little protection against the cold. The heavy fullness of bodies is indicated by a skillful, painterly handling of texture and drapery.

The bright tonality and local colors of Rembrandt's early pictures (soon to be abandoned) were still reminiscent of Lastman; for example, the grey-blue, yellow and red of Anna's kerchief and the bright salmon-pink of Tobit's mantle. But the light grey of Anna's dress and the cool greenish grey of the background show a tendency toward monochrome, thus making the red-yellow glow of the fire doubly effective as it casts warm highlights over figures and animals. Now begins that masterly interplay of light and shadow which Rembrandt, here too starting out from Caravaggism, studied chiefly in interiors and developed into the main dramatic vehicle of his painting. Over and above these tokens of his precocious technical mastery, however, stands his deep sense of humanity: how moving is the helpless grief of the blind old man, how impressive Anna's indignation at her husband's doubts as to her honesty! Granting that the whole composition may derive from a work of the Haarlem painter Buytewech, the fact remains that in the expression of character and psychological motivation Rembrandt owed nothing to anyone. *Tobit and Anna* is but the first of a long series of works illustrating the simplest, most touching story in the apocryphal books of the Old Testament.

How deeply Caravaggesque realism impressed itself on the young Rembrandt is demonstrated by many other pictures as well, by *Christ driving the Money Changers from the Temple* (Pushkin Museum, Moscow), for example, with its turbulent half-length figures. Such early works betray a certain crudeness and even downright shortcomings in the composition. Figure groups still produce the effect of having been fitted together piecemeal; at the same time, however, they are imbued with a naïve grandeur that does not shrink from defects and

*Musical Company, 1626. Rijksmuseum, Amsterdam.*

discords in order to attain the full expression Rembrandt is aiming at. That he was acquainted with the work of the Utrecht Caravaggeschi is proved by a remarkable painting of 1626 (Rijksmuseum, Amsterdam) showing his family making music: Rembrandt at the harp, his father at the cello, his sister singing, his mother listening, all fantastically clad in oriental and old-fashioned Netherlandish costumes. This, together with the *Justice of Brutus*, is the first sign of his predilection for subjects taken from antiquity, for the exotic and remote, which was so characteristic of Late Mannerism in Holland, but which in Rembrandt's work was finally sublimated into the universal expression of an imaginative world of vivid poetry. Rembrandt did not set out to paint a group portrait; the familiar faces of those dearest to him served only as the starting point from which his vision evolved. Reality was always the indispensable springboard of his imagination. For type figures of varying ages his father, mother, brothers and sister posed repeatedly in these early works. Thus the model presumed to be his father appears by candlelight in the *Money Changer* of 1627 (Berlin), a nightpiece reminiscent of Honthorst. The essential feature here, however, is not so much the figure as the beautifully painted still life of books and parchments. Rembrandt had seen such still lifes as these, symbolizing the vanity of earthly things, in the works of the Leiden painter Pieter Symonsz. Potter and they must have stirred a desire to emulate them. Evident in much of his early work is his delight in the still life, in old weapons, vases and folio volumes. His eye drank in forms and colors greedily, transforming the visible world into painterly sensations.

Besides figuring in single, highly expressive portraits (Mauritshuis, The Hague; Windsor Castle), Rembrandt's father and mother also served as models for the great biblical characters. As imposing and statuesque as the pillar beside her, his mother personifies the prophetess Hannah standing over the devoutly kneeling group around the Child in the *Presentation in the Temple* (Hamburg). The pyramidal composition of the Italians is built up like a tower into the heights. This

*The Presentation in the Temple, ca. 1628. Kunsthalle, Hamburg.*

soaring verticalism which, countervailing the ponderous, earthbound bulk of figures, emerges as the second formal tendency in Rembrandt's early works, may have been derived from Jan Pynas. At the same time the brightness reminiscent of Lastman, which we noted in the work of 1626, went out of his colors now as he turned increasingly to the broken tones that enhance the chromatic richness of monochrome harmonies. Here too the influence of Pynas may be detected. Greenish-grey and rust-brown, earth colors, wax-yellow and brownish-red flesh tints, together with broken white and grey in the surrounding architecture, are massed around the intense greenish blue of Mary's mantle. Henceforth he worked in terms of broken and inflected tones. The *Flight into Egypt* (1627, Tours) is bathed in moonlight that virtually blots out local colors. Rembrandt called increasingly on color to transmit light, thereby depriving it of all material significance.

While the flowing brushstroke of 1626-1627 still smoothly models forms in the traditional manner of fifteenth and sixteenth-century painting, by 1628-1629 he had moved on at one bound to an almost rhapsodic boldness and freedom of touch. The speed with which he progressed is phenomenal. In etching too he achieved from the very first the acme of perfection. His unrivaled grasp of line and draftsmanship—in many ways the key to his art—was the instrumental factor of this rapid evolution. For all its unassuming simplicity, the *Supper at Emmaus* in the Musée Jacquemart-André is perhaps the loftiest, noblest creation of Rembrandt's Leiden period, and it shows to what degree mastery in the handling of light can transform and spiritualize matter, can effect a "transubstantiation"—which is in fact the esoteric theme of this small panel.

This is a candlelight scene of the type so often painted by the Utrecht Caravaggeschi, but what an extraordinary change from their custom-bound banality! The figure of Christ screens off the source of light, which throws up a pale, silvery yellow aureole behind the mysterious presence. The rest of the picture is submerged in tones of deep grey and loam-brown, so that the glimmer of the candle gains immensely in brilliance and seems to emanate from Christ's transfigured body like a magic flame. The visionary power of this apparition makes itself felt in the hastily sketched features of one disciple, dazzled by the light, while the other, swallowed up in the gloom, has fallen at the Savior's feet and with the curve of his back initiates the powerfully rising diagonal which culminates in Christ's majestic head. This is immeasurably superior in expressive power to the picture Huygens

*The Supper at Emmaus, ca. 1629. Musée Jacquemart-André, Paris.*

praised so warmly, that of the repentant Judas returning the thirty pieces of silver (Marchioness of Normanby Collection), a Bible scene containing several figures, famed for its truthfulness of gesture and action. But Rembrandt at his simplest, as in the *Supper at Emmaus*, is Rembrandt at his best and greatest. Such a work is an extraordinary performance for a young man in his early twenties, who in the roughly contemporary self-portrait, *The Artist in his Studio* (Museum of Fine Arts, Boston), seems to be engaged in a dialogue with a panel still on the stocks, standing behind the huge easel that fills half the picture. Here too the monumental effect is heightened by the simplicity, indeed the starkness of the composition. How eloquently this small picture testifies to the passionate industry of the young painter, alone in his large, empty studio, oblivious to everything except the work before him.

Rembrandt portrayed his own features more frequently than those of anyone else. No other artist has left us so many self-portraits, most of them dating from his early and late periods. In the early self-portraits he studied his own face chiefly for its capacity to register and hold varieties of expression under changing lighting conditions. Often he deliberately exaggerated the plebeian cast of his features, but he also painted into them his spiritual tension, his ennobling awareness of his creative powers, notably in the Mauritshuis *Self-Portrait*, where the rosy cheeks full of the melting softness of life strike so strange a contrast with the dark iron-grey gorget he has donned for the occasion. Compared with the works of 1626 the tender, mellow modeling of this head comes as a surprise, every hint of linearism having vanished. Saturated in rich highlights, colors are so smoothly blended that nowhere can distinct limits be set to zones of color. No less smooth and vaporous is the way the head dissolves into surrounding space; it seems to stand there like the cloudy condensation of some mysterious fluid.

As early as 1628 this fundamental change had begun to come over Rembrandt's way of seeing. Figures stand no longer as separate entities, distinct from the space around them, but are intimately bound up with that space which, like an undulating mist or fluid, washes over them

*David Playing the Harp before Saul, 1630.*
*Städelsches Kunstinstitut, Frankfurt.*

in a ceaseless crescendo and decrescendo of light, so that they tell out like a crystallization of that fluid. This is why their pictorial reality is conveyed far more positively and palpably than is the case with other artists who set out from the idea of an abstract plastic volume which they proceed to clothe in colors. Herein lies the magic of Rembrandt's much-admired chiaroscuro, which has exerted so great an influence.

We find it first in *Samson and Delilah* (1628, Staatliche Museen, Berlin), a simply conceived yet highly dramatic work. We see it fully developed in *Saul and David* (Städelsches Kunstinstitut, Frankfurt), in which, with exquisite artistry, the painter uses thin glazes of color—low-toned wine-red, greenish silver-grey, and discreet accords of blue and yellow (the very color-chord that later meant so much to the Delft school) —as a sounding board for light.

*St Paul, ca. 1630. Germanisches Nationalmuseum, Nuremberg.*

Like the Utrecht painters, Rembrandt in his Leiden years applied himself to the study of old men and women, bent and furrowed with age, first in drawings, then in etchings and paintings of the same models. To begin with, he rendered them with the frank realism we find in the character studies of the Utrecht school. Soon, however, he rose above the commonplaces of reality and, thanks to his masterly handling of light-drenched color, these familiar figures underwent a poetic transfiguration. He transformed them into prophets, visionaries, apostles, defenders of the faith, who pursue their biblical soliloquies before our eyes. Thus Jeremiah amid the ruins of the Temple, mourning the destruction of Jerusalem (1630, Amsterdam), is bathed in an unearthly light that seems like a reflection of the burning city. (To get such effects Rembrandt often let the red-brown ground preparation of his panel show through, or scraped down to it through the wet pigment with the handle of his brush; the picture then seemed to glow from within, as if steeped in some fiery substance.) Thus St Paul sits lost in thought over the Scriptures, his venerable figure caught in two conflicting streams of light: the yellowish glow from an unseen lamp behind the large open book on the table, and a cool natural light pouring in from the upper left. Gleams of fiery pink play over his left hand and on his robe. Warm and cool tones alternate harmoniously in the fabrics: golden tan on his robe, blue-grey on sash and sleeves, deep violet on the tablecloth. This tissue of colors, however, serves but one purpose: to distribute the light-accents that emphasize the spiritual content of the work. The left hand rests on the table in full light, tense with the vehemence of his thoughts, while the right hangs down in shadow, limp, inert. The texture of the pigment varies from a heavy, granular impasto to thin glazes, everywhere adjusted to bring out the message of the picture (note how the swords re-echo all the colors in brief flashes).

The extraordinary thing about these meditative figures is the way in which Rembrandt uses the dramatic play of light to deepen the religious import of the picture. Even his own mother becomes an

*Rembrandt's Mother, 1631. Rijksmuseum, Amsterdam.*

*The Presentation in the Temple, 1631.*
*Mauritshuis, The Hague.*

apparition from the ancestral past when he portrays her as a prophetess or sibyl, as in the spellbinding painting (1631, Amsterdam) where we see her bending over the Bible, whose shining pages reflect a soft golden glow upon her shadowed face. Admirable too is the symphony of colors that rises out of her velvet cloak: full or muted according to the consistency of the pigments, red-lake in the depths of the folds, violet-pink on the edges, a cool bluish grey in the fur neckpiece, old-gold and silver in the headdress. By some miracle of color this visionary presence arises out of shadow into light, and a mood of awed suspense descends on the beholder, as if he had crossed the threshold of a sanctuary.

That mystery-laden atmosphere of a sanctuary is found again in the *Presentation in the Temple* (1631, The Hague). The scene is set in a cathedral, whose unfathomable vaults tower into far-flung heights.

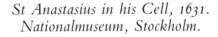

*St Anastasius in his Cell, 1631.*
*Nationalmuseum, Stockholm.*

*Self-Portrait with a Gorget, ca. 1629. Mauritshuis, The Hague.*

Their vastness is brought home to us by the tiny figure group caught in a ray of light coming down upon them from an upper window like the beam of a spotlight, and throwing the brightness of the Christchild, light of the world, into contrast with the gloom of the synagogue, symbol of the dark world of the Old Dispensation. No other artist since Van Eyck and the early German masters had so tellingly rendered the awe-filled atmosphere of a church interior. The grandeur and poetry of his vision of space link up Rembrandt with his great predecessors of two centuries before. Dürer's and Altdorfer's versions of *St Jerome in his Study* stand as the immediate forbears of the Stockholm interior of 1631 known as *St Anastasius in his Cell*. Like a cool, blue-grey mist, light floods in from the open window, playing on the golden yellow walls of the vaulted chamber. As always with Rembrandt, the masonry seems to have grown out of living stone, untouched by human hands, as a result of natural erosion. The architecture in his pictures is always medieval—Romanesque or Gothic—while its decoration consists of elements deriving from the earshell and cartilage ornament of the Late Renaissance. Frankly reverting to the past, he breathes new life into bygone forms and makes no attempt to create a "modern" architecture, as Rubens had done with Baroque forms.

With a tremendous increase of expressive power by means of chiaroscuro, and with the creation of a new pictorial microcosm, Rembrandt's Leiden period came to a close. In Amsterdam new and very different tasks awaited him.

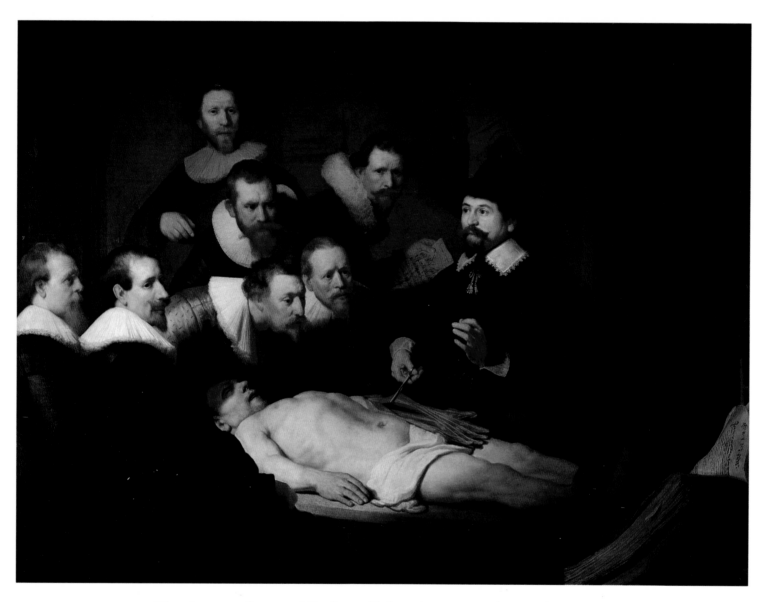

*The Anatomy Lesson of Professor Tulp, 1632. Mauritshuis, The Hague.*

# MANIERA GRANDE
## THE EARLY AMSTERDAM PERIOD

I N AMSTERDAM Rembrandt felt impelled to move on from the small formats of his Leiden period to those larger works whose presentation reflects the tendency of the age toward what the Italians called "la maniera grande"—the Grand Manner. Hence the large-sized canvases that now take the place of the small wooden panels and copper plates on which he had painted hitherto. The *Holy Family* of 1631 (Alte Pinakothek, Munich) is the first sign of this change of style, which led to the series of life-size portraits of Amsterdam patricians. With these Rembrandt entered into competition with the well-established Amsterdam portrait painters Thomas de Keyser, Nicolaes Elias and Dirk Santvoort, whom he soon excelled in their own special field.

The most significant work of 1632 is his group portrait of the *Anatomy Lesson of Professor Tulp* (Mauritshuis, The Hague). Such corporation portraits were a national speciality in Holland, and their evolution has been traced in a penetrating study by Alois Riegl, which also throws essential light on Rembrandt himself. They were commissioned by learned societies, craftsmen's guilds, charitable institutions and Civic Guard companies—of which there were a great many in

Holland—to decorate their club rooms and meeting halls. These collective portraits were an expression of the democratic spirit of the nation, each figure being given equal prominence in the picture. The subordination to a leader of outstanding personality is entirely voluntary, and such is the case with this group of university students attending an anatomy demonstration by their professor. While in previous Amsterdam portrait groups there is always something stiff and constrained about the figures, Rembrandt succeeded in linking them together and breathing organic life and unity into them. They form not only a well-constructed, well-balanced pyramidal composition in the spirit of Italian art, but also a psychologically unified group listening attentively to Professor Tulp's lecture.

New possibilities in the field of the group portrait were thus opened up, possibilities that had far-reaching effects on Rembrandt's later work. For the time being, however, as a result of this success in a difficult undertaking, he reaped an immediate benefit in the form of numerous portrait commissions, which flowed in steadily during the 1630s and which he filled with skill and gusto to the entire satisfaction of his sitters. Particularly impressive are the full-length portraits of married couples, such as those of Maerten Soolmans and Oopje Coppit (Rothschild Collection, Paris) and of Elison, pastor of Norwich, and his wife (Boston), both of 1634. Usually the man looks out at the spectator, to whom he presents his wife, doing so with a dignified, yet candid and natural gesture that is much more direct in its appeal than the proud aloofness of Van Dyck's aristocrats. This of course is a general characteristic of Dutch painting, particularly conspicuous in the masterly portraits of Frans Hals, but Rembrandt's men and women radiate a warmth and personal intimacy which he alone was able to breathe into his pictures.

In addition to these commissioned portraits we find a large number of figure paintings made for his own satisfaction: venerable old men in fanciful dress, oriental costumes or priestly vestments (*The Noble Slav*, 1632, New York; *Oriental*, 1633, Munich; *Turk*, Washing-

*Portrait of Saskia, 1633. Gemäldegalerie, Dresden.*

ton; *Rabbi*, 1634, Prague), or comely women in rich velvets and furs adorned with pearls and jewelry. After the auburn-haired girl, presumably his sister Lijsbeth, who appears so often in individual portraits up to 1632 (Stockholm), came the long series of magnificent paintings of Saskia in which Rembrandt extolled the beauty of his young wife. It begins with the society portrait, still "official" and ceremonial in mood, that dated from the early days of their acquaintanceship (1633, Musée Jacquemart-André, Paris). Soon, however, he was attiring her in precious fabrics, showering her with fabulous jewels, making her seem

*Artist Drawing from a Model, 1639. Graphische Sammlung Albertina, Vienna.*

*The Prodigal Son, ca. 1635. Gemäldegalerie, Dresden.*

like an enchanted apparition out of some poetic dreamland far removed from the workaday world. In the Cassel and Dresden portraits (1633) he shows her sumptuously gowned as a lady of fashion of Lucas van Leyden's day—another token of his constant predilection for everything relating to the past. His delight in the splendors of color transported him into the realm of the visionary. Jewels, finery and purple velvets seem to glow from within. The broad-brimmed hat of the Dresden portrait casts a shadow over Saskia's smiling face, so that her golden complexion, her strawberry-red lips and rosy cheeks lie partly in brightest light, partly in shadow dappled with surface reflections. Rembrandt handled light not in accordance with reality but in accordance with his free imagination, although he exactly observed all the tonal values of reality. Borne on a ray of light, this graceful image of a happy wife rises out of fiery darkness. At other times he decked her out in the poetic guise of Flora, the flower goddess (Kauffmann has pointed out literary parallels in the works of the "Muiderkring" poets). Thus we find her, naïve and unaffected despite the splendor of her costume, in the Hermitage portrait of 1634, in which she wears a green silk, gold-embroidered mantle, while red, white and green-blue flowers weave a many-colored garland around her dark hair and pink-cheeked face. We find her again, but majestic and imposing now, even more gorgeously attired, in the London *Flora* of 1635, from which we get the impression that the model was studied in blazing sunlight, while the rest of the picture is plunged in fathomless darkness—a perfectly irrational light effect, carried to its extreme in the *Night Watch*.

A master in rendering man's image, Rembrandt was equally great in rendering action, whether human or divine. There has never been a greater interpreter of the Bible, whose episodes he illustrated not only in countless drawings and etchings but in a long series of paintings. He painted these pictures in response to an inner need, and out of a desire to penetrate and interpret the message of the Old Testament and the Gospels. Calvinist Holland had no use for the religious paintings for

*Portrait of Saskia as Flora, 1634. Hermitage, Leningrad.*

*The Raising of the Cross, ca. 1633. Alte Pinakothek, Munich.*

which there was so constant a demand in the Catholic countries. The result was that the devotional picture ceased to exist, its place being taken by the historical picture illustrating biblical episodes. The admiration of the Protestants for the Israelites of the Old Testament, who maintained their faith in *one* God in the face of heathen persecution, was as strong in Calvinist Holland as it was in Puritan England, each nation likening its own historical role to that of the Chosen People.

This being so, painters in Holland tended to represent Old Testament scenes more frequently than subjects taken from the New Testament, and to specialize in small-sized pictures serving to decorate sacristies, parochial offices and private homes. His teachers had painted many such pictures and Rembrandt followed suit—but with a difference. His instinctive understanding of Christ and the Christian doctrine of love for one's neighbor and redemption was so total, so deeply rooted in the warm humanity of his own nature, that the Gospel stories occupy a much larger place in Rembrandt's work than in that of other Dutch painters.

Shortly after his arrival in Amsterdam he received a commission of this kind from the Stadholder, Prince Frederick Henry, thanks to the good offices of his friend and well-wisher, Constantijn Huygens, private secretary to the Prince. Originally for a *Raising of the Cross* and a *Descent from the Cross*, the order was later enlarged, at his patron's desire, so as to include a complete Passion cycle, intended of course not for a church but for an art lover's private home. This great Passion cycle, formerly at Düsseldorf in the collection of Duke Johann Wilhelm von der Pfalz, is now in the Alte Pinakothek, Munich. The letters Rembrandt wrote to Huygens in connection with this commission have been preserved. The pictures, five in number, are all of small dimensions; a drawing shows Rembrandt at his easel working on one of them. Two decades earlier Rubens had also interpreted the Passion of Christ in his gigantic altar paintings for Antwerp Cathedral. Rembrandt must have known these works through prints, for he obviously strove to produce something comparable to them, but different in kind.

*The Large Raising of Lazarus, 1632. Bibliothèque Nationale, Paris.*

*The Descent from the Cross, 1633. Rijksmuseum, Amsterdam.*

Borrowings from Rubens appear in the *Raising of the Cross*: the pyramidal group of men in mid-picture straining to raise the heavy Cross, also the captain on horseback towering up beside them. But here, instead of Rubens' powerful diagonal, the composition is marked by a sharp upward drive, a flame-like aspiration heavenward, which recalls the expressive verticalism of Late Gothic. The top of the picture, like the altar paintings of the sixteenth century, is given the shape of a semicircular arch. The oppressive darkness of an approaching storm weighs on the scene; only the Crucified is lit up by a pale stream of light. An intensely personal vision takes the place of Rubens' epic breadth of treatment.

Rembrandt himself figures prominently among the soldiery raising the Cross; thus he is an accessory to the crime against the Savior, but the expression on his face shows that he is fully conscious of that guilt. Heart-stricken, he takes part in the tragic event. The fact is that Rembrandt projected his own thoughts and feelings into the Bible story so unreservedly that never, before or since, has the personal, subjective element been carried so far in Christian art. The semicircular panel acts as a window through which we watch the scene taking place. The innocent captain looks out at us with a pained expression of reproach, mutely accusing us all of the crime he is being compelled to commit, while the painter rivets his eyes on the crucified Christ.

A similar interpretation is given to the *Descent from the Cross*, executed in the same year, whose form reverts to the stylistic idiom of Gothic, though its visionary conception is intensely personal. Here too Rembrandt himself, overcome with remorse and compassion, helps to lower the body of the Lord from the Cross. Both panels down to the last detail are painted with the painstaking exactitude and delicacy of a miniaturist; in this respect they conform to the old tradition of the Late Gothic court painters, differing completely from the broad brushwork characteristic of all Rembrandt's other work in the thirties. The execution of the three remaining panels of the Passion cycle, which were probably commissioned immediately after delivery of the first

*The Descent from the Cross, ca. 1633. Alte Pinakothek, Munich.*

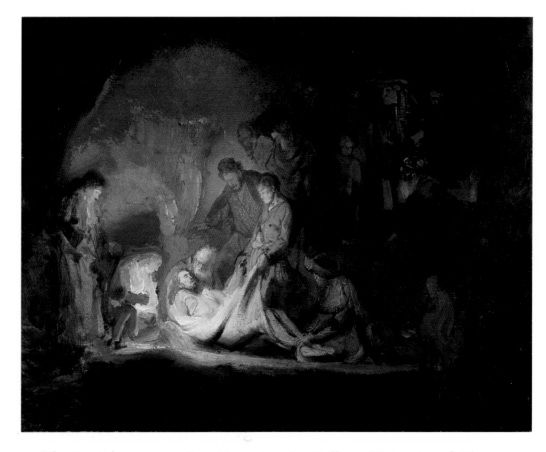

*The Entombment, ca. 1633. Hunterian Art Gallery, University of Glasgow.*

two, proved to be a long, exacting task; finally completed in 1639, this cycle of paintings stands out as the major achievement of the decade 1630-1640. Years elapsed between Rembrandt's first conception of these pictures and the date of their completion.

The *Ascension* (1636) and above all the *Resurrection* (1637) are full of dramatic movement, while the *Entombment* strikes a softer, quieter note. The first two pictures retain the cool tonality typical of the early thirties: wax-yellow, pale blue, pink and a discreet gold-green, embedded in a somber ash-grey. While the cool tones of the *Ascension* fade into pale gold, the *Resurrection* is all aflame with gold and fiery reds. Rembrandt had already interpreted the theme of the Entombment in a small grisaille (University of Glasgow), datable to about 1633, which anticipates essential features of the main figure group in the Munich *Entombment*, and in fact may well have been a preliminary study for it made after the Prince of Orange asked him to complete the Passion cycle. And though only a study, this small work is remarkable for the way Rembrandt, with a minimum of pictorial means, realized everything he set out to express: the silent anguish of the mourners around the dead Christ, whose agony is so poignantly conveyed, with a few strokes of the brush, by the face now relaxed in death. In this "grautje," as the Dutch call these small pictures in grey monochrome, the shadowy human forms seem like a condensation of atmospheric space. It is precisely in this self-imposed limitation of his means that Rembrandt most clearly reveals his greatness. The contrast between the cool grey shadows and the ruddy golden glow of the torch brings out an indescribable wealth of tonal values.

The expression of movement—of the "beweechgelickheyt" which he prided himself on having achieved in the *Resurrection* (letter to Huygens, January 12, 1639)—was the great problem that engrossed him in this decade. This dynamism, generated by cross-currents of emotional tension, dominates not only the religious paintings (*Ecce Homo*, 1633, National Gallery, London, and *Christ calming the Storm at Sea*, 1633, Isabella Stewart Gardner Museum, Boston) and the etchings (*Raising of Lazarus* and the *Annunciation to the Shepherds*, 1634), but also the mythological pictures such as the *Rape of Europa* (1632) and the *Rape of Proserpina* (Staatliche Museen, Berlin). The dramatic expression of movement is carried to its highest pitch in the last-named painting which, however, is still imbued with all the subtlety and finesse of Late Gothic and Late Renaissance art forms, as evidenced by the enchantment of the landscape and the fantastic, microcosmic vision reminiscent of Altdorfer and Elsheimer. This dynamic movement led in turn to increasingly monumental form, a trend that reached its climax about the middle of the decade. It was in the thirties that Rembrandt came closest to the so-called Baroque style which at that time reigned supreme not only in Italy but also in Flanders, France and Spain. By

1635 his art could vie with that of the Italians for grandeur and power. This did not involve any overt imitation of their practice; he had simply developed a deeper sense of monumental form, the logical consequence being that he turned increasingly to larger formats. For this his life-size portraits doubtless prepared the way. Dutch art had always had an innate tendency toward passivity and immobility. Never before had it known such turbulent movement as Rembrandt now developed in his large-scale biblical and mythological compositions. The picture space is filled with massive, stalwart bodies actuated by a rhythmic movement all in sweeping curves; objects appear to be either dropping to earth or flying through the air. He delighted in seizing on moments of high tension, dramatic suspense or imminent catastrophe: Abraham just as the angel stays his upraised arm, so that the knife falls from his hand and Isaac's life is spared (1635, Leningrad); Ganymede as a terrified child, struggling desperately as Zeus in the form of an eagle carries him aloft (1635, Dresden). In the contemporary drawings we see Christ staggering under the weight of the Cross, Jacob filled with horror at the sight of Joseph's blood-stained coat, the Virgin Mary slipping down from her seat as the angel of the Annunciation appears before her.

This stylistic change was not merely a new adaptation of Italian art as revealed through the mediation of Dutch artists who had been to Italy. It was brought about by a firsthand study of the Italian masters themselves. Rembrandt passionately sought out such works of theirs as could be found in Amsterdam, and through the medium of Baroque he instinctively went back to the sources of that style: the great creations of the High Renaissance. A drawing in the Albertina after Raphael's *Portrait of Baldassare Castiglione*, which Rembrandt made during an auction sale in Amsterdam, shows the eagerness and thirst for knowledge with which he pursued these ends. The sight of a mediocre print of Leonardo's *Last Supper* was enough to enable him to grasp the nobility and grandeur of the original, which he had never seen, and to recreate it in a work of his own, the wonderful pen-and-

*The Rape of Ganymede, 1635. Gemäldegalerie, Dresden.*

*Study for* The Jewish Bride, *1635. Nationalmuseum, Stockholm.*

*The Hundred Guilder Print, ca. 1642-1648. Bibliothèque Nationale, Paris.*

ink drawing in Berlin. The revelation of Leonardo's great fresco continued to take effect on him long afterwards: in *Samson's Wedding Feast* (1638, Dresden), the *Hundred Guilder Print*, the Louvre *Supper at Emmaus*, and even in the *Julius Civilis*.

Rembrandt was able to study movement in the works of the great Venetians from Titian to Tintoretto, and the Central Italian painters from Correggio to Lelio Orsi. These masters were all represented in his collection of drawings and prints. But though he felt keenly attracted to the Italian masters of the High and Late Renaissance, Rembrandt could never bring himself to make a break with the Caravaggism which had meant so much to him in his youth.

The truth is, rather, that Caravaggio came to assume fresh importance for him as he undertook to integrate the free expression of movement, which he had now fully mastered, into the effective rendering of visual reality, always one of his constant concerns—to fuse them into a unified whole. What mattered to him now was not so much the painterly quality of the picture or the surface texture of objects as the sheer physical bulk and palpable, plastic solidity of powerful bodies in dramatic conflict with each other. This was his essential concern in the large figure paintings of 1635-1636: *Belshazzar's Feast* (National Gallery, London) and the *Blinding of Samson* (Frankfurt). The latter spares the beholder none of the horror of a violently realistic scene; here indeed, letting himself go, Rembrandt achieves all the *terribilità* of Caravaggio himself. It is a wild mêlée of giant bodies, so arranged that they form an inverted pyramid. There is often something strange and mask-like about the figures in Rembrandt's historical compositions; here this applies in particular to the soldiers, who in many respects resemble the queer, goggle-eyed figures in so many of Bruegel's paintings. They express all the blind stupidity of brute force. Like some demonic sorceress, her foul deed accomplished, Delilah runs toward the light with Samson's hair in her hand, and against the dusky red of the halbardier the spectral blue of her skirt glimmers like an ignis fatuus.

But Rembrandt did not persist in this clangorous fortissimo. In the following year, with the *Angel Leaving the Family of Tobias* (1637, Louvre), he resumed that series of small cabinet pictures in which he concentrated the tremendous resources of his imagination on a strictly limited surface, whose dramatic and poetic possibilities he fully explored thanks to his grandiose vision of space, which is suggested rather than defined. The movement in the Louvre picture springs not from

*The Blinding of Samson, 1636. Städelsches Kunstinstitut, Frankfurt.*

physical violence, but from the emotional reaction to a miraculous event. A cloud floats up like a puff of smoke and opens out in a zone of unearthly light into which the angel glides away, like a celestial dancer, while over those who remain on earth there hovers an aura of incorporeity, of flame-like spiritual ardor. The terrestrial and the

*The Angel Leaving the Family of Tobias, 1637.*
*Musée du Louvre, Paris.*

heavenly commingle, just as do the brilliant golds and dusky shadows of the chiaroscuro. Rembrandt's conception of movement had been lifted to a spiritual plane.

The beautiful *Noli me tangere* (1638, Buckingham Palace) seems to vibrate with the holy joy of Eastertide. A friend of Rembrandt, the poet Jeremias de Decker, wrote the simple, touching verses on the back of this small panel. The Holy Sepulchre opens on a fragrant garden sparkling with the early morning dew—exactly the atmosphere so movingly evoked in the Resurrection music of Rembrandt's great contemporary Heinrich Schütz. The first rays of the sun are playing on the distant towers of a cathedral above the cool, blue-green depths of the park, and tinting the edges of the Sepulchre with a salmon-pink sheen. The white gardener's tunic worn by Christ has an unearthly pallor in the pale golden dawn; it is the symbol of light, identifying Christ with the rising sun. Wrapped in a dark purple cloak, Mary Magdalen tarries in the shadows; only her face is illuminated by the growing light. So far as color is concerned, this is the finest picture painted by Rembrandt in the 1630s. Though it recalls Grünewald and Altdorfer, its color effects are even subtler, more evanescent and fluid, than those in the Resurrections of the early German masters. We are tempted to speak of a color alchemy, a mysterious transmutation of one substance into another—yet there is no violation of the laws of nature.

Landscape had always had its place in Rembrandt's backgrounds. By the late thirties, however, both in his etchings and paintings, it had begun to assert itself as a picture element in its own right. The landscapes in the paintings are with few exceptions composite landscapes, products of his imagination. Grandiose and fantastic, they had their predecessors in the landscapes of Hercules Seghers, who in his own day and milieu had led as solitary a life as Rembrandt. Seghers' rockbound mountain prospects are like glimpses of the world after the Deluge, or of some dead planet pitted with extinct volcanoes. Their forlorn grandeur and desolation made a very strong impression on Rembrandt in his youth, and these are the qualities we find in his early landscapes, most powerfully expressed in the *Stormy Landscape* (Brunswick). Strewn with the ruins of an old town, a mountain rises in terraces above the broad floor of a valley. A river swirls in cascades under an old bridge and flows into the plain. While the composition still owes much to the tradition of Elsheimer's Dutch followers, how different is the spirit of his composition! A threat of cosmic catastrophe seems to brood upon the scene. The sky is covered with grey storm clouds through

*Stormy Landscape, ca. 1638. Herzog Anton Ulrich Museum, Brunswick.*

which here and there break slanting shafts of eerie light, illuminating patches of the countryside. Here again is Rembrandt's "irrational" chiaroscuro. The dark outlines of the bridge stand out against a spectral burst of light. Sallow green and grey alternate with deep shadows, while the golden ground color shines through in the foreground, rendered in light, fluid brushstrokes. This landscape gives us a glimpse of the visionary world of a great poet. It is useless to look for the charming details that delight us in the landscapes of the naturalistic Haarlem painters, Jan van Goyen, Pieter Molyn and Salomon van

Ruisdael, who for the sake of atmospheric unity often employed a similar monochrome tonality; here is nothing but a majestic plainsong, the voices of the cosmic powers.

Rembrandt painted few landscapes, but in them he surpassed even the best of his Dutch contemporaries, some of whom were landscape painters of the first rank. It was the custom in Holland for painters to specialize in the portrait, the still life, the interior, landscape, or the genre scene. Rembrandt alone mastered all these fields, thanks to the richness and universality of his imagination, and in each he far excelled all his coevals. The best Dutch colorists had been inspired by the glistening plumage of a dead bird standing out against a neutral

*The Three Trees, 1643. Bibliothèque Nationale, Paris.*

*Self-Portrait with a Dead Bittern, 1639. Gemäldegalerie, Dresden.*

ground, but Rembrandt's *Self-Portrait with a Dead Bittern* (1639, Dresden) leaves them all far behind. Dressed as a hunter, the artist is stepping from the shadows and holding up his kill to the light, as he proposes to hang it on a hook. The incidence of light calls up a whole symphony of colors in the bird's plumage; a counterpoint of tones flashing out of the cool grey, the warm smoke-brown and brown-golden white, with fiery red accents in neck and head. Only Goya and Manet proved capable of painting a dead bird with a like command of painterly and tactile values, but even they could not surpass him. Here we have perception transfigured by the loftiest creative imagination. The colors take on a rich, grainy texture in the feathers, whose downy softness they so perfectly convey that we seem to feel it under our fingers. Rembrandt was the first painter in the history of art to work so directly with the impasto and exploit so skillfully the physical properties of his medium, yet no other artist has spiritualized the *matière* of the picture as he did.

*The Triumph of Mordecai, ca. 1641. Bibliothèque Nationale, Paris.*

# THE NIGHT WATCH

TAKEN all in all, the 1630s may legitimately be described as Rembrandt's "Baroque" period, in which, as a successful artist, he won full recognition from the best society of a great metropolis, yet never deviated a hair's breadth from his self-chosen path. Then, with the beginning of the forties, all the ostentation went out of his work; there was an end to the spectacular demonstrations of his almost superhuman creative powers—superhuman, yet steeped in so deep and intense a feeling for the human. Rembrandt suddenly revealed himself in a new light. He showed increasing interest in architectonic values, first as thematic material in their own right, then as a means of pictorial construction. About 1640 he made some sketches after views of old English cathedrals and towns. In the biblical paintings of that year, such as *Abraham dismissing Hagar* (Victoria and Albert Museum, London) and the *Visitation* (Detroit), architecture plays an important part, and an even more important part in the etchings: the *Presentation in the Temple*, the *Beheading of John the Baptist*, the *Triumph of Mordecai*. The heaven-aspiring vertical compositions of the late thirties give place, for the most part, to well-balanced compositions in breadth. In them architecture plays a part not only in the concrete sense of the word, but also in the figurative, for what we find here is an *architecture of light* resulting from the fusion of figural composition with an immanent light-rhythm which, while it does not actually conflict with natural light phenomena, fails to provide any naturalistic motivation for them.

After reverting entirely to small picture formats toward the end of the thirties, Rembrandt now turned again to gigantic canvases in which figures are fully integrated into the irrational space-magic of his chiaroscuro. He was more and more inclined to pit himself against monumental problems, such as those encountered in *Manoah's Sacrifice* (1641, Dresden), a large-scale work of sacramental gravity. During this time Rembrandt must already have been working on his most famous and popular painting, the one with which his name is chiefly associated: the *Night Watch*, completed in 1642. It owes its celebrity not only to the fact that it is a very unusual picture, but also to the well-known fact that with this work Rembrandt made a drastic break with contemporary taste and thus aroused the hostility of the public; this was the beginning of the end in the material sense, his first step on the downward path that led to the ultimate catastrophe.

Portrait groups of Civic Guards, the so-called "Doelen," had been a common feature of Dutch painting since the sixteenth century. These volunteer defense units had played an heroic part in the long wars of religion and independence which the Low Countries had waged against Spain, but in Hals' and Rembrandt's time they had ceased to serve any military purpose; they were now little more than social clubs whose members, dressed in showy uniforms, met periodically for shooting practice, parades and banquets. Frans Hals' banquet pictures are a particularly colorful and festive expression of the civic spirit animating these groups of burgher-guardsmen. The guild of the Harquebusiers (*Kloveniers-Doelen*) ordered from Rembrandt a work whose size far exceeded that of Hals' banquet pictures, a work showing the men—all painted life-size—marching out in full dress.

*The Night Watch (The Sortie of Captain Frans Banning Cocq's Company), 1642. Rijksmuseum, Amsterdam.*

The *Night Watch* is not only Rembrandt's most famous and popular picture, but also the one which, both in his lifetime and after his death, aroused the most criticism. Later generations were uncertain what to make of this theatrical display of mimic warfare and this strange light breaking through the darkness. Hence the misnomer "The Night Watch," although it has always been obvious that the light playing over the main figures is sunlight; this has been made even clearer by a recent cleaning. Moreover, documents have been published, enlightening us as to the history and meaning of the picture. The family album of Frans Banning Cocq, captain of the company, contains a watercolor copy of the picture with the following inscription: "Heer van Purmerlandt (i.e. Frans Banning Cocq) as captain gives orders to his lieutenant, Heer van Vlaerdingen (i.e. Willem van Ruytenburg), for the Civic Guard to march out." It was a festive occasion that had brought the militiamen together: the state visit to Amsterdam in 1637 of Marie de' Medici, queen mother of France. All the Civic Guard groups in the city paraded out and took part in the festivities. Hence the tumult and apparent confusion of the company which, assembled in loose formation, is still awaiting the order to "Fall in." Only the captain and lieutenant are getting into line. The men have just come through the dark vault of the city gate and are emerging into full sunlight. The arrangement of the figures is similar to that in the contemporary etching of the *Triumph of Mordecai*. After lowering their banners and lances so as to pass under the low archway, the men are raising them again as they come out into the open. Other guardsmen load or inspect their muskets. The drum is sounding, orders are ringing out. A high-spirited soldier boy has just fired off his flintlock musket behind the captain and an older trooper prudently thrusts the barrel aside. Children are pushing their way through the crowd, dogs are barking excitedly. It is just such a scene of general confusion as the painter must have noticed many times in the streets of Amsterdam. Yet all this noise and bustle is kept under control and, indeed, almost stifled. The result is very different from all other Civic Guard pictures.

A contemporary copy of the *Night Watch* by Gerrit Lundens (National Gallery, London) shows that the canvas was later cut down on the left side, with the loss of two figures and the view of an arched bridge. The large figure of the captain, dressed in black with a dark red sash across his breast, originally stood in the exact center of the picture, thus assuming a dominant position unusual in Dutch corporation pieces.

In an Italian painting the archway here would have described an exactly symmetrical span above the captain; not so with Rembrandt, whose compositional rhythms always have something asymmetrical or syncopated about them. The small lieutenant, Willem van Ruytenburg, would cut an insignificant figure beside his chief, were it not for the bright yellow of his uniform gleaming in the sunshine. The embroidery of his coat and the embossed work of his armored throat-piece are modeled in golden yellow pigment so thickly laid in that it seems to have been sculpted in low relief with the handle of the brush. A second beam of light is focused on the little girl, whose features recall those of Saskia. There is something unreal and ghostly about her as she glides into the midst of these stalwart militiamen. Here the flood of yellow light is lemon-hued and glistens on the sea-green silk of the mantle flung over her shoulders. Color is bodiless and spiritualized. Hanging from the girl's waistband is a white cock with grey-blue plumage; this is the symbol (the "klauwklove") of the "Doelen."

The rich color scheme of the *Night Watch* is heightened beyond anything to be found in the earlier works, yet all colors are subdued. The young soldier firing off his musket is an extraordinary tissue of grey, blue, red and dingy yellow. The deep red of the man on the left loading his musket glows with a phosphorescent sheen. Cool colors such as blue, green and olive-green (the ensign, the drummer's sleeve) are counterbalanced by warmer tones (the honey-colored golden ochre of the drum). Dark areas consist of a deep golden brown and a purplish black-brown with a tinge of red in it.

*David's Farewell to Jonathan, 1642. Hermitage, Leningrad.*

The play of light in the picture is unquestionably the fruit of an observant, step-by-step study of reality. These incoming shafts of sunlight, these reflections, half-shadows and dimly lit pools of darkness all come directly from nature. This is not the diffused light of the open air, but the light that Rembrandt could always control and regulate by opening and closing the shutters of his studio. He was no open-air painter, though he could have been a very fine one, as the charming

*Winter Landscape with Ice Skaters* (1646, Cassel) proves. But neither is this a uniform or rational interior lighting; rather, an arbitrary distribution of light effects, scattered here and there, a combination of a sunlit interior with a fog-bound, overclouded landscape, as in Rembrandt's heroic landscapes of fantasy, with their lowering storm clouds, or his grisaille of *John the Baptist preaching in the Wilderness* (Berlin), in which the light ebbs and flows in softly throbbing waves, obeying no laws but its own. The effect is to bathe the scenic elements in the unreal atmosphere of a dream.

Alois Riegl, discussing the *Night Watch*, likens the crowd of men behind the two officers to a landscape background of the kind we see in *David's Farewell to Jonathan* (1642, Leningrad), a magnificent picture not unlike the *Night Watch* in color and atmosphere. Clad in a knee-length coat of golden silk girdled with a pink sash, David sinks into the arms of Jonathan (whose features are those of Rembrandt himself). The color harmony of pink and blue stands out against the grey mists rising in the sky beyond, just as the two officers stand out against the dark background of the city gate. The *Night Watch*, like the landscapes, is not an image of banal reality but a drama of light sublimated into a world of dreams. Few of the figures wear the costumes of the period, as Frans Hals' officers do. Besides the apparel fashionable in the sixteenth century and the days of the Spanish wars, we find firearms, headpieces and armor that had gone out of use long before Rembrandt's time. So capricious, so arbitrary is Rembrandt's choice of costumes and accessories that one writer has ventured to suggest that these people were on their way to a masquerade. What is more, Rembrandt completely disregarded a basic principle of the corporation portrait: that each member of the group should be equally visible to the beholder. Instead of a portrait, Rembrandt produced something midway between an historical painting and a life-size genre piece. Thus in paying for the work, for which Rembrandt charged 1,600 guilders, each member of the company contributed according to the prominence given him in the picture.

Riegl made a masterly analysis of the picture's artistic and historical significance in the evolution of the Dutch group portrait. Compared with the works of the previous decade, the *Night Watch*, like *Manoah's Sacrifice* shortly before it, shows Rembrandt laying greater stress on the plane of relief, which he boldly cuts through by means of orthogonal projection, with the result that the plane surface of the canvas is seemingly transformed into three-dimensional space. The two officers in the foreground, Cocq and Ruytenburg, the latter with a foreshortened pike in his hand, are walking directly toward the spectator. And though they take no notice of him, they advance so resolutely in his direction that his instinctive reaction is to step aside to let them pass. Thus he gets the feeling of being directly involved in the action of the picture, and even though no one apostrophizes the spectator (as is the case in almost all other group portraits) a deeper communion is established between him and the scene represented.

At the same time the picture has the greatest possible inner unity because, we feel, this throng of people had inevitably to be represented in just this way and no other. It is the same inner unity that Rembrandt had already achieved in the Berlin drawing of Leonardo's *Last Supper* and in *Samson's Wedding Feast*. Also in the *Night Watch* the lesson learnt from the great Florentine is manifest. This led Riegl to feel that, here, Rembrandt carried the Italian principle of subordinating secondary elements to the point of doing violence to the Dutch principle of co-ordinating all parts of the picture; the leading figure, in his opinion, is inordinately prominent. But in 1635-1636 Rembrandt came closer to Italian Baroque art and its subordination of the picture unity to a *single* dominant element than he did in the *Night Watch*. And this was accepted by his contemporaries, with respectful surprise but without withdrawing their approval from the artist. There must have been other reasons why they took exception to the *Night Watch*.

What Rembrandt had done was to turn an official portrait into an exercise of the creative imagination, on which he trained an eye accustomed to penetrating beneath the surface of things. Though he gave a masterly rendering of the material aspects of the picture, of weapons and garments, he also rendered the immaterial aspect, the psychic undercurrents of the scene. An example: over the lefthand group of guardsmen floats an eerie bluish light, resembling moonlight and contrasting with the warm sunshine of the central part of the picture. The last man on the left sits on the parapet of the (unseen) bridge; his face is modeled in a waxen yellow-grey, above which glitters the grey-blue helmet with gold-embossed dragons on it. As it so happens, we know that soon after the picture was finished this man died; here, as if Rembrandt had seen into the future, his figure produces the uncanny effect of a revenant, like the ghost of Hamlet's father on the battlement of Elsinore. No man, either then or now, would want to see himself portrayed in such a manner.

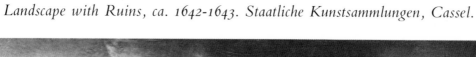

*Landscape with Ruins, ca. 1642-1643. Staatliche Kunstsammlungen, Cassel.*

The painter having put so much of himself into a work in which he was expected to observe the rules of objectivity, the men commissioning it found themselves before a *fait accompli*. There was of course an attenuating circumstance: Saskia's death had thrown his mind into a turmoil and in concentrating on the visionary element he was seeking a relief from his sorrow. But those who came to him for their portraits desired no visions other than that of their own features faithfully mirrored. In default of this, they were led to reject the work and turn elsewhere.

No painted sketches for any of Rembrandt's pictures are known to exist. The making of such studies was foreign to his conception of art, and he preferred to work out the picture directly on the canvas itself. Sometimes, however, when preoccupied with a particular idea, he interpreted it in different works produced at about the same time. Thus we find the figure groups of the *Night Watch* foreshadowed in the *Concord of the State* (Rotterdam), a monochrome painting dated 1641.

Mention has been made of the "landscape" nature of the chiaroscuro effects in the *Night Watch*. The same period saw Rembrandt experimenting with dramatic light effects in the *Landscape with Two Bridges* (Philips Collection, Eindhoven), *Landscape with Three Trees* (1643) and *Landscape with Ruins* (Cassel). This last picture heralds the calm that was about to come over Rembrandt's manner of composition. Not without reason has a parallel been drawn with Claude Lorrain's landscapes. Out of the depths of golden twilight rise the terraced slopes of a mountain landscape, culminating in a temple-like edifice. The contrasts of the chiaroscuro are balanced by the transfigurative power of Rembrandt's light. Here he seeks everything restful, vast and equilibrated that the motif can give him, emphasizing the right angles formed by verticals and horizontals. We find a similar procedure in the landscape drawings made from nature in the course of the 1640s.

This new calm and profundity also affected Rembrandt's figure compositions, and his religious paintings of the middle and late forties

*The Holy Family with Angels, 1645. Hermitage, Leningrad.*

are characterized by an atmosphere of silent awe and devout introspection. They illustrate not the great historical events of the Bible, but the toilsome, care-laden daily life of the Holy Family, including however those memorable moments of quiet happiness and intimacy that light up every home. All the simplicity, human warmth and loving-kindness of which the heart is capable imbues the *Holy Family with Angels* (1645, Leningrad). Joseph bends over his carpentry work in the faint, red-

*The Holy Family, 1646. Staatliche Kunstsammlungen, Cassel.*

golden glow of the fire burning in the hearth. Mary is a young girl, hardly more than a child, the image of a purity and innocence befitting the "handmaid of the Lord." She turns for a moment from the Bible to the cradle, unaware of the celestial light softly streaming down upon her and the angels on noiseless wings gliding above, worshipful and protective. (Little Titus served as model for the foremost angel.) The gorgeous Rembrandt red of the cradle's coverlet, the golden yellow of its foxskin lining, the cool white of pillow and sheet, the deep copper-pink of Mary's dress—all illuminate the scene. Once again Rembrandt stresses local colors, but they remain vehicles of light. The

Child sleeps on peacefully and happily. An idyll of love and solicitude, unwitting of its grandeur, blends with the tidings from a higher world to form a unified whole of the simplest, tenderest kind. The idea of religious faith sanctifying our daily life in a workaday world is expressed to perfection in this picture. Furthermore, purely pictorial qualities not being taken as an end in themselves, there results a deeply human directness and immediacy of artistic statement, even affecting form, that shows Rembrandt's art taking a new direction.

If an even more intimate and personal interpretation of the Bible story is possible, Rembrandt achieved it in the Cassel *Holy Family* of 1646. He painted a frame around the scene and screened part of it off behind a painted curtain. Thus he represented not reality but a picture. Or better, he represented two realities on different planes: the outer and the inner reality, into which anyone who contemplates a work of art must gradually be drawn. The spectator is presented not only with a picture, but with a picture within the picture. For *him* the curtain is drawn aside. Though the scene may be likened to a stage, it is a theater intended for an audience of one—you or me or anyone else who, exercising his privilege, draws the curtain aside for a moment—but softly, so as not to intrude on the hallowed stillness in which, amid the evening shadows, Mary sits beside the fire, holding the Child close. This infinitely tender light, mild as a moonbeam, issues not so much from the tiny fire as from the Virgin and Child themselves. The gathering dusk creates an atmosphere of dedication and devoutness —the essential message and content of the picture.

About the same time Rembrandt painted an *Adoration of the Shepherds* (1646, Munich) whose atmosphere is very similar, and a *Circumcision of Christ* commissioned by Prince Frederick Henry of Orange to complete his Passion cycle.

The most important testimony we have of the change coming over Rembrandt is a canvas painted in 1648, of modest dimensions but full of an inner grandeur: the *Supper at Emmaus* in the Louvre. The arrangement of the figures is derived from Caravaggio, whose violent

*The Supper at Emmaus, 1648. Musée du Louvre, Paris.*

realism, however, has vanished without leaving a trace behind. The faultless symmetry of the figure group, which is developed on the picture surface, shows that Leonardo contributed quite as much as Caravaggio to the composition. The importance of the tectonic elements is obvious from the staging of the scene: bare, massive architecture rises high above the figure group, which is closely framed between two pilasters, while the vaulted niche behind Christ is filled with mysterious shadows. Like the figures, the architectural elements do not recede but adhere to the picture surface, not filling it symmetrically but —as always with Rembrandt—thrown to one side in a movement of syncopation, thus loosening the strict symmetry of the rest of the composition. The picture surface is not impenetrable as it is in Italian art. Faintly tinted with gold, red and green, the moldering walls seem to palpitate in the radiance emanating from Christ, and become a transparent medium through which we perceive depths of space. Thus this surface relief, while apparently closing off the space beyond, nevertheless conveys the sensation of spatial recession far more strongly than the vaulted halls of Rembrandt's earlier works. The secret of his later work is that of expressing spatial depth in terms of purely surface effects, produced by the condensatory power of color, light and atmosphere.

The face of Christ—related to the face of the model used by Rembrandt for the Christ of the *Hundred Guilder Print*—is in fact that of a man who has known unspeakable suffering and met death. This is the most human vision of Christ that art has ever given us. The gestures of the disciples are full of restrained, silent emotion. A lifting or a clasping of the hands expresses more than all the monumental pathos of Italian art. Late in life Rembrandt preferred the quiet and intimate stories of the Bible to the more dramatic ones. With the Louvre *Supper at Emmaus* we reach the most significant turning point in his artistic evolution. The "Holy Year" of 1648 marks the threshold of his maturity and brings us within sight of the sublimely moving art of his old age.

*Girl at a Window, 1651. Nationalmuseum, Stockholm.*

# UNUM NECESSARIUM

## MATURITY AND LAST YEARS

> When in matters of art it is asked what is most
> needful in a picture, the reply is: "Just as in life the
> eye apprehends the object seen, so it must also be
> able to recognize the object painted in a picture."
> However fine the colors may be, however much
> this or that ornamental accessory may enhance the
> work, these add nothing to the essence of the thing.
> And so it is in all things: the essential must be
> distinguished from the incidental, the necessary
> from the unnecessary. When the distinction is not
> made, confusion arises.
>
> Johann Amos Comenius, *Unum necessarium*
> (chapter III, *Ars artium*), Amsterdam 1668.

IT was the Rembrandt of the period 1630-1650 who was redis-
covered and so much admired in the eighteenth century and by the
Romantics. The Rembrandt of the 1650s and 1660s is the man who,
since Impressionism, has been hailed as the supreme master of European
painting. It was the art of Goya and Manet that led to the recognition
of this Rembrandt, who was revealed to us by the expressionist movement of our own generation. For us today the great Rembrandt is the
later Rembrandt, the creator of a painting which for elemental power
has no equal in art history, a painting which bursts through the barriers
of the temporal world and enters a realm of absolute and timeless
validity. There can be no doubt that this art, expressing everything in
an elemental language of color, had a special significance for Rembrandt. He knew that his contemporaries would have difficulty in
following him all the way. His correspondence with Huygens shows
that even in the early days he wished his pictures to be viewed from
a distance, and Houbraken reports that in his old age Rembrandt
discouraged visitors to his studio from looking too closely at his
canvases, saying: "The smell of the paints will disagree with you!"

*Portrait of an Old Jew, 1651. Formerly Devonshire Collection, Chatsworth.*

Though the art of his maturity and old age is free of those elements of the unusual and extravagant which, up to the *Night Watch*, had baffled his contemporaries, it was no more accessible to them now than before. The reason lay in his mode of expression. Though we may regard Rembrandt in this respect as a precursor of the moderns, the fact remains that for him the creation of a new style of pictorial representation was not an end in itself, but a means to an end. Contemporary witness accounts refer again and again to his fidelity to nature.

Of course this was an attitude that held good for all the masters of Dutch naturalism. The period 1650-1670 was the classical age of Dutch painting, and mastery of composition, space, atmosphere, color and light reached its peak in the work of Pieter de Hooch and Vermeer, Philips Koninck and Jacob van Ruisdael, Jan van de Cappelle and Emanuel de Witte, Terborch and Kalf. Yet their work is very different from Rembrandt's. What Rembrandt understood by "nature" was a kind of reality implicit in the picture and arising from an inner truth and necessity of which no previous painter had had any conception. Of this the study of his mature and late works has much to tell us.

From 1650 to 1655 Rembrandt produced his greatest etchings, and produced them more abundantly than ever before. To this period date his wonderful landscape etchings and the Bible scenes including the large Passion plates. At the same time his creative energy overflowed into a great many drawings. As a result of this *furor graphicus* his production of pictures naturally declined to some extent. The painter was marking time, mustering his forces. Except for a few biblical pictures with small figures in the lineage of the *Supper at Emmaus*, we find hardly anything but portraits. And these with few exceptions are portraits of freely chosen models, such as Rembrandt had painted as "studies" in his youth. Now, however, they are carefully thought-out likenesses, mostly in half length, of individual people dwelling in the world of their own thoughts. Here begins the leading theme of Rembrandt's lifework: man in himself. Between these portraits and those of his youth there are hardly any grounds of comparison. Then he had been attracted by what was particularly realistic or picturesque in a model, anything striking or out of the ordinary, and he had rendered it even more striking by unusual lighting or costumes from the rich store of "properties" in his studio; now he let the human face speak for itself and disclose an inner realm of silent thought and spiritual depths. He still made frequent use of the outmoded costumes which he had always been so fond of and which transported his models back into the distant past, as in the wonderful *Portrait of an Old Jew* (1651,

Chatsworth), but he used them now without the ostentatious splendor of his earlier period, without those sumptuous effects of color and texture. To the profoundly introspective gaze of this pale face, the cold sheen of an ermine neckpiece, relic of bygone splendor, plays the part of a discreet accompaniment, and nothing more. The effect is to make the suggestive power of color greater than it ever was in the past; we see this in the patch of red, glowing in the light, on the shoulder of the cape, the old-gold of the chain, the glints of fiery red and golden brown in the shadowed head of the animal whose fur covers the old man's chest. Tones are deeper and warmer, richer and more sonorous than before.

We know that late in life Rembrandt often preferred the company of simple people, with whom he could relax and be himself, to the cultured circles in which he had formerly moved. Among these people he found some of his most congenial models. A young servant girl employed in his house, hardly more than a child, now shy and distrustful, now friendly and confiding, inspired him to works that number among the finest pieces of pure painting that Rembrandt ever produced. In a painting of 1651 (Washington) we see her with the attributes of her household duties, broom and scrub-bucket, leaning over the low wall around a well and gazing gravely toward the spectator. The picture is as simple, straightforward and humanly convincing as it can be. The whole attitude of this young girl makes us feel that she takes her duties seriously. The canvas is painted with a broad brush, and beautifully done. Chardin himself could not have made a finer still life of the broom and overturned pail, nor Manet better have conveyed the green- and gold-tinged white of the sleeves standing out against a bodice of cinnamon red. An even greater triumph of pure painting is the Stockholm picture of the same model (1651), in which the auburn-haired girl, her head propped on her arm, leans on the window sill and looks at us with amiable indifference. The color of her jacket is that deep-glowing terracotta red of which Rembrandt in his maturity was so fond. With the ivory white of her blouse

*Old Woman Seated, 1654. Hermitage, Leningrad.*

and the deep black of the background we come to that simple, basic color scheme out of which the later Rembrandt, like the later Titian, built up most of his pictures. The brushwork is broad, the impasto thick and creamy. Patches and planes of color weld the picture elements indissolubly together, yet do so with a mellowness and delicacy unequaled by any subsequent painter except Cézanne.

Although the physical texture of the color is more strongly brought out than ever before, it is at the same time powerfully vitalized

*Man with a Gilt Helmet, ca. 1652. Gemäldegalerie, Staatliche Museen, Berlin.*

and sublimated. In his portraits and single figures Rembrandt ventured further with his new technique than in other works: the result is a tissue of broad, bold brushstrokes and color patches laid in with the palette knife, of tremulous lights painted in with the half-dry brush, of modellings and rubbings made with the bare fingers. The finest of these portraits is the *Man with a Gilt Helmet* (Berlin). That open texture familiar to us in the drawings and etchings is here carried over into painting. The face is shrouded in penumbra. The brownish grey under-painting—used now in place of the fiery-red bole-color with which he had previously prepared his canvases—everywhere shows through the network of brushstrokes, rubbed over with a half-dry brush and thus rendered transparent. The man sinks into shadow, while inert matter —the gold helmet with its patterned relief work done in thick impasto—comes vividly to life in brilliant light. Despite the lavish working of the pigment, the glittering helmet fails to remain a material thing, but is spiritualized and elevated to the same plane of higher life as that of the shadow-darkened face. In Rembrandt's later work matter and spirit are but the outward manifestations of an inner essence at the heart of things. The model for this picture, who sat not only for a whole series of paintings but also for the etching *Dr Faust*, is presumed on good—though not decisive—grounds to be Rembrandt's brother Adriaen.

In filling the portrait commissions of his youthful period he had often composed companion pictures of married couples; so now, taking the models of his choosing, he brought them into spiritual harmony with each other. The pensive figure of an aged Jew in a picture at the Hermitage seems to form a pendant to the wonderfully spiritualized portrait of an old woman (both 1654), who for no valid reason has been identified with Hendrickje's mother. (This canvas, also in the Hermitage, has been enlarged at the bottom and on either side; originally the figure was posed far more solidly and monumentally in the frame.) The old woman, whose face, bearing the imprint of a deep understanding of man's fate and all its sorrows, calls to mind the Norns

*Self-Portrait Drawing by a Window, 1648. Rijksmuseum, Amsterdam.*

of northern mythology, may well have reminded Rembrandt of his own mother and her air of a venerable prophetess; profoundly moved, he sounded the depths of that face and made visible its inner light.

Rembrandt's portrait-painting reached its climax in the likeness of his friend Jan Six, whose date is given by the sitter himself in a

*Woman with Child Descending the Stairs, ca. 1636. Pierpont Morgan Library, New York.*

chronogram as 1654. This is the greatest of all his single portraits. Rembrandt had long been friendly with the young poet and humanist, scion of one of Amsterdam's most distinguished patrician families. He had already portrayed him in 1647 in one of his finest etchings. Six was a great art lover and undoubtedly one of the few who could follow Rembrandt's later development with insight and understanding. So that in this portrait Rembrandt not only gave expression to all his natural affection for a close friend, but handled the painting in his own way with uninhibited freedom—which he could hardly have done in the case of any other portrait commission. He constructed this memorial to a friendship as he saw fit, following the dictates of his own temperament. Plying a broad brush, he covered the canvas with the most amazing piece of alla prima painting in the history of art. Over his dark grey coat with pale golden-yellow buttons, whose color is re-echoed in the gloves, Six has thrown a mantle of the most magnificent Rembrandt red, with an ochre yellow lapel. Then comes the creamy white of the collar and the black of the hat (once again the Titian palette). The shrewd, worldly-wise look in his eye—he was thirty-six at the time—makes him seem much older than his years. His attitude is as unaffected, as free and natural as possible. He has just come in from the street and, entering his friend's studio, is taking off his gloves and cape. Thus Rembrandt observed him, and thus revealed his innermost being.

With this work Rembrandt achieved the full splendor of his mature style. The experience and discipline gained in the drawings and etchings of the early fifties had now ripened into sovereign freedom and mastery. Rembrandt had attained the Titianesque heights of his art. Like the drawing-pen, the brush obeyed the subtlest motions of his hand; the breadth and sweep of his touch reveal the presiding genius of a master mind in full control of form and matter. Rembrandt's fame as a painter now equaled his fame as an etcher, but it was greater abroad than in his own country. In 1654 Don Antonio Ruffo, a Sicilian nobleman living in Messina, acquired from Rembrandt a portrait of

*Portrait of Jan Six, 1654. Six Foundation, Amsterdam.*

*Aristotle before a Bust of Homer, 1653. Metropolitan Museum of Art, New York.*

Aristotle (1653, Metropolitan Museum). As he grew older Rembrandt showed increasing interest in the art of classical antiquity and the High Renaissance. His own collection of antiques included a copy of a Hellenistic bust of Homer; from 1652 on this moving effigy of the blind poet made so strong an appeal to his imagination that we find it recurring under varied guises in many works, even in biblical scenes. In 1652, in the family album of his friend Jan Six, he made a drawing of *Homer on Mount Parnassus* in which he took inspiration from Raphael's fresco in the Stanza della Segnatura.

In the *Aristotle* we see the philosopher lost in meditation, in silent colloquy with the bust of his great exemplar. The figures who people Rembrandt's later works inhabit a spiritual realm of their own, that self-contained private world so well described in the words of that great thinker and educator Comenius: "Man contains within himself everything that forms a part of his being, no part of his being lies outside himself, he is self-enclosed as, for example, a circle or a sphere. Therefore man best finds himself within himself, and nowhere else. Thus also he will find both God and the world within himself." The dark-bearded philosopher of pallid mien, a man with oriental, almost Slavic features who so often served as Rembrandt's model in the last, lonely years, contains within himself a vast, sublime world of his own. His fanciful costume is medieval rather than antique. On night-black velvet he wears a gold chain—such gold as no one had ever painted before, lavishly molded in fully plastic relief, yet elusive as tongues of flame. Even the deep folds of his sleeves are transformed by light into gold. He personifies the medieval conception of Aristotle as the great magus of antiquity, the pillar of scholasticism, the fountainhead of all knowledge. This ideal portrait of the great pagan philosopher merges into that of the Christian apostle Paul. This is not the last time we shall meet with this union of paganism and Christianity in the all-embracing humanity of Rembrandt's later work.

The close parallel between Rembrandt and Titian in their maturity has often been remarked on. Instead of bold effects of spatial

*Portrait of Hendrickje Stoffels as Flora, ca. 1653.*
*Metropolitan Museum of Art, New York.*

recession we find in Rembrandt's later work a broad deployment of the composition and figures on the picture surface, which, however, is organized as an optical plane, saturated with atmosphere and connected with the surrounding atmospheric space by means of vibrant contours. The difference is made clear by a comparison of his early versions of *Flora* with the later ones. About the same time as the *Aristotle*, and using the same amply folded linen drapery, Rembrandt painted Hendrickje as Flora (New York). How simple and tonically calm is the effect of this picture beside the pomp of the London *Flora*! Instead of a frontal pose we have a classical profile. The composition

*Woman Bathing, 1654. National Gallery, London.*

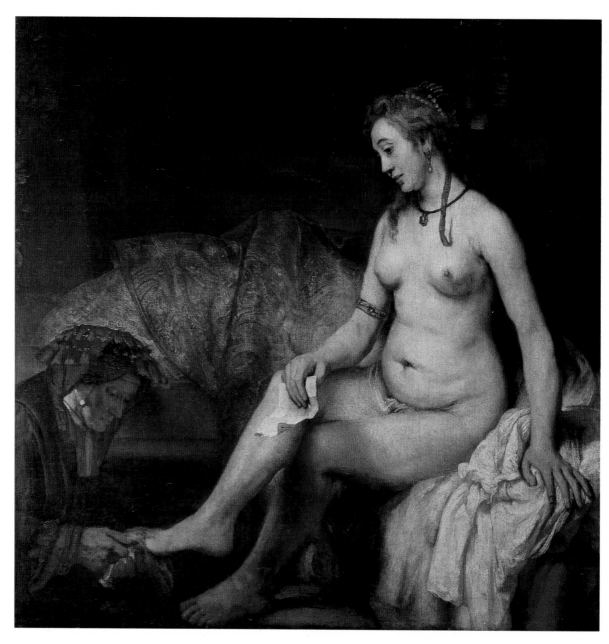

*Bathsheba, 1654. Musée du Louvre, Paris.*

was undoubtedly influenced by Titian's *Flora* in the Uffizi, which is known to have been in Amsterdam in Rembrandt's time. Yet how much more human and psychologically penetrating seems Rembrandt's *Flora* beside the distant, inaccessible idealism of Titian's.

Rembrandt's female nudes of 1654 represent an absolute of painting that, before him, only the great Venetian can be said to have attained. They are the equal of Titian's nudes for sheer mastery in rendering the physical texture of naked bodies glowing with golden light and pulsing with the breath and blood of life; they are superior to them in the rendering of atmosphere—which with Rembrandt signifies a spiritual fluid. The *Woman Bathing* (1654, London) exemplifies the admirable simplicity and breadth of Rembrandt's brushwork, which models form so delicately and firmly; the arms and thighs, for instance, smooth planes of pale gold running between dark, vibrant contours. These flesh parts contrast beautifully with the cool, grey-shadowed white of the shift, while the gold and the somber purple of the garments she has laid on the bank behind her kindle faint gold reflections in the dark mirror of the water. The color harmonies of his previous work seem poor beside the bewildering richness of this scale of tonal values. More impressive still, for its gorgeousness and introspective intensity, is the great Louvre *Bathsheba* of 1654, for which Hendrickje also posed. Bathsheba at her toilette has just received King David's letter and falls to brooding on it, while an old servant-woman dries her feet. Her uncertainty of mind and the conflict of warring impulses going on within her are poignantly suggested by the expression on her face; the shadow of a tragic destiny has fallen over her. Thus, into the art of Rembrandt's maturity, there comes a kind of psychic chiaroscuro, complementing the optical chiaroscuro. This picture has much to tell us of Rembrandt's fully developed methods of composition. The nude figure is developed strictly in terms of the picture surface, and even the crossing of the legs is so calculated as to avoid any undue emphasis on three-dimensional space; it is expressly left to alternate zones of light and shade alone to situate the figure in space, and these suffice to do so far more effectively than the earlier use of volumetric projection. Again the harmony of grey, red and gold: the bright, ivory-skinned nude with grey shadows rippling over her, the cool white of her linen streaked with blue-grey shadows, the dull red of the bench, and the gold of her mantle smoldering like fiery embers. Beads glitter in her dark hair and a dark-red ribbon falls across her throat.

The youth in shining armor with the owl-figure helmet of Pallas Athena (1655, Glasgow) recalls the fact that Rembrandt painted an *Alexander the Great* which, together with the magnificent *Homer* (1663, The Hague), he made to the order of Don Antonio Ruffo and sent to Messina; these formed a triad with *Aristotle with a Bust of Homer*—the great philosopher, the brilliant young soldier he tutored, and the man both of them revered as the greatest epic poet of all time. Built up in flakes of color that glow like cooling lava, the idealized portrait of Homer is uncannily alive, and the sightless eyes with the mysterious luster of a gold Mycenaean mask seem to conjure up the very soul of archaic Greece; but it was too much even for Rembrandt's Italian admirer, who failed to appreciate the picture and, regarding it as unfinished, sent it back to the artist. This gave rise to an exchange of angry letters in Italian. Ruffo, however, remained loyal to Rembrandt and continued his purchases, the last of which, a large set of etchings, was shipped from Amsterdam in 1669; by the time they reached Messina Rembrandt was in his grave. The Glasgow *Alexander*, with its shining lights on polished armor, seems to be a prefiguration of the *Julius Civilis*.

It is often claimed, quite wrongly, that Rembrandt had no genuine feeling for antiquity. Proof to the contrary is provided not only by the pictures just mentioned, but by a whole sequence of other works. One of the finest of these is the *Polish Rider* (Frick Collection). The man portrayed is thought to have been an officer in the Lysowski regiment. But this bold, exotic-looking horseman, riding through the dusk in a hilly landscape, is the very image of the nameless hero, a seeker and a wanderer through the world—like so many of Rembrandt's models. Once before, in the late forties, he had done a life-size equestrian portrait, of the merchant Frederik Rihel, a work that still conformed to the usual Baroque type of equestrian portrait. Here we have

*The Polish Rider, ca. 1655. Frick Collection, New York.*

something totally different. Rider and horse are entirely enclosed in the truncated pyramid of the landscape background. The dying light of sunset kindles red and golden gleams on rider, saddle and harness. The horse stands out in sharp relief, reduced to an ash-grey phantom that brings to mind Mörike's *Feuerreiter*. At the same time it breathes an underlying classicism, with its bony structure modeled to the apparent consistency of marble; its ancestors are the horses of the Parthenon frieze. Such is Rembrandt's Hellenism: created out of his own resources, but reaching across the centuries to renew contact with the greatest achievements in the history of art.

In addition to these poetic visions, however, Rembrandt also recorded the familiar scenes of his day-to-day life in pictures of equal depth and psychological intensity. We see little Titus (1655, Rotterdam) sitting over his school work or drawing with a pen, a look of earnest concentration on his face, his large dark eyes dreamily gazing into the distance, his pale complexion shining out against the autumnal red, subdued green and deep tones of the surrounding twilight. In the Munich picture of Hendrickje her dress is brushed in with such broad fluid strokes that it seems transformed into a cascade of liquid gold.

In the *Flayed Ox* (1655, Louvre) we have the paradigm of pure painting. The theme was not a new one, having long been used as an element of the still life; we find it in the sixteenth century in the work of Aertsen and Beuckelaer. But Rembrandt handled it in monumental fashion, giving it a cosmic amplitude. Hanging on stout thongs in a butcher's cellar, the carcass acquires an illuminating power of its own and emits an iridescent sheen in the semi-darkness. Pigments are condensed into pure light, streaming with gold and different hues of red: brick, salmon, cinnamon, crimson, pink. In Rembrandt's hands a gutted carcass becomes a treasure chest of sparkling jewels.

Having successfully overcome all the difficulties involved in the vast body of graphic work he produced from 1650 to 1655, Rembrandt seemed to turn with renewed powers to the specific problems of painting. And his new solutions of these problems led to monumental

*The Flayed Ox, 1655. Musée du Louvre, Paris.*

*The Anatomy Lesson of Dr Joan Deijman, 1656. Rijksmuseum, Amsterdam.*

pictures with life-size figures; thus began the last and mightiest phase of his painting, which gained in depth and power uninterruptedly to the end of his career. After 1661 there are no more etchings, and drawings too become rare. The spiritual process that before had found an outlet in these techniques henceforth took effect exclusively on canvas. Brushwork and coloration evolved in the direction of ever greater freedom. He combined boldness and magnitude with a subtlety and finely shaded differentiation that far transcend the careful chiseling of detail characteristic of earlier periods. As hitherto in the drawings, now in the paintings he embraces the whole gamut of expression, from the tenderest, most fleeting intimations to the massive convulsions of huge forms built to the dimensions of the fresco. All his resources are directed to a single end: the expression of spiritual essences. This led in turn to a material enrichment of the picture substance that gives the later paintings an opulence and density of texture exceeding anything to be found in the earlier work.

The deep humanity and earnestness, the compelling truthfulness and objectivity, of the style of Rembrandt's old age resulted in a new influx of portrait commissions, which had become rare indeed in the intervening years since the *Night Watch*. In 1656 the class studying under the surgeon Dr Deijman ordered a group portrait from him for the Amsterdam School of Anatomy. This work is a painted critique of his first *Anatomy Lesson*. Unfortunately, as the picture was destroyed by a fire from which only a fragment was salvaged (Amsterdam), we have to refer to the small preliminary drawing to get an idea of the original work. The presentation was strictly tectonic and symmetrical, with the professor, seen frontally, carrying out his demonstration in the exact center. The students, seated on the benches of the anatomy amphitheater of Amsterdam University, are disposed in equal numbers on either side of him. The corpse is stretched out before the surgeon in much the same abrupt foreshortening as Mantegna's *Dead Christ* in the Brera. The compositional principles of Rembrandt's late style are here clearly developed and the fragment preserved is one of his most powerful, most arresting creations. The professor is dissecting the brain. An assistant stands beside him, holding the top of the skull; his expression is one of silent awe in the presence of death. What grips the beholder in the present state of the picture is the face of the dead man, with its somber, frozen expression of ineffable tragedy. On it is graven all the distress of mankind confronted by the brevity of life. Beside the spiritual grandeur and almost sacramental restraint of this work, the *Anatomy Lesson of Dr Tulp* has the air of a society portrait.

With *Jacob Blessing the Sons of Joseph* (1656, Cassel) Rembrandt created one of his great classical works. It is a painting full of mature wisdom, exquisite color and spiritual insight. The theme is the blessing given by Jacob on his deathbed to his grandsons Ephraim and Manasseh, whose parents, Joseph and Asnath, stand by looking on. Icono-

*Jacob Blessing the Sons of Joseph, 1656. Staatliche Kunstsammlungen, Cassel.*

graphically, the picture is related to the theme of Isaac blessing Jacob so often treated by Rembrandt and his pupils. Thus the main lines of the composition had been laid down long before. While using the Caravaggesque device of the half-length figure group, Rembrandt brings the figures compactly together and develops them uniformly on the picture surface. The foreshortening of the bed beneath the dark-red blanket, indicated by the gleaming bedposts, is sharp and bold, yet made unobtrusive by an immediate return to surface patterning in the main figure group. The rite of blessing is hallowed by an atmosphere of hushed solemnity.

While the early Rembrandt delighted in painting moments of decisive physical action, the later Rembrandt preferred those sudden revelations of psychic tension that called for psychological insight into human nature—a gift he possessed in the highest degree. His eyes dim with age, Jacob gives his blessing to the younger boy, while Joseph gently intervenes, trying to move his father's hand to the head of the firstborn son, dark-haired Manasseh. But Jacob refuses, for he knows that God's favor is with Ephraim, whose sweet and innocent features are suffused with a shimmering golden light. It would be impossible to represent the Bible story (Genesis 48) more simply, nobly and significantly than Rembrandt has done here. The spiritual climax of the scene is indicated clearly and simply: the contact of the two hands above Ephraim's head. Joseph's figure, seen slightly in recession, is veiled in a mist of glancing shadows. Essentials are brought to the forefront, the rest is shrouded in darkness. The children's mother, Asnath, an Egyptian princess, is portrayed in the costume of a lady-in-waiting at the court of Burgundy; a brass statuette designed by Jan van Eyck for the tomb of Louis de Mâle served as model for this figure. In this noble, awe-inspiring work oriental antiquity and the Christian Middle Ages enter into mysterious communion. The brush alone, Rembrandt found, was not enough to spiritualize the figures to the degree he desired, and large portions of the canvas are built up directly with the palette knife. Hence the cloud-like, floating effects of surfaces, the vibrant patchwork and broken iridescence of the color.

In the following years the material conditions of Rembrandt's life progressively worsened until finally he was declared bankrupt—an event that would have crippled the efforts of any other artist. The loss of time alone—time that otherwise would have been devoted to creative work—must have been incalculable. But his creative powers

*Self-Portrait, 1659. National Gallery of Art, Washington.*

*Self-Portrait with Brushes, Palette and Maulstick, 1660. Iveagh Bequest, Kenwood House, London.*

were so great that they lifted him above it all. We can see the tragic effects of this struggle for bare existence in the change that comes over the self-portraits which now followed one another in close succession year after year: a self-confession and a statement of accounts. In the features of the 1657 *Self-Portrait* (Earl of Ellesmere) are mirrored the reverses and disillusionment of that unhappy year, but nothing more could ruffle the Olympian calm of the great *Self-Portrait* of 1658 (Frick Collection). In that of 1659 (Washington) his hair has turned grey and though the fifty-three-year-old artist seems to stand on the threshold of old age, the fire glows unquenchably beneath the ashes. In the 1660 *Self-Portraits* (Louvre, Kenwood House) we find a leonine Rembrandt, sorely stricken, with his white painter's cap on his grey head, committed to the struggle to survive, his face telling not only of affliction and resignation but also of wisdom and kindliness. He carries a whole world within himself. "Just as each separate man is a self-contained world, with his own heaven and earth, with fire and water, mind and matter, light and darkness, movement and rest within himself, so the entire history of mankind ordained by God is mirrored in each man" (Comenius, *Unum necessarium*, chapter VI).

At the beginning of the 1660s Rembrandt's late style evolved toward a grandiose monumentality. It was now that he painted the great historical pictures in which the grandeur of outward form is only equaled by the loftiness of the spiritual message. The significance of this new monumental painting, of which the *Denial of St Peter* (1660, Amsterdam) is an outstanding example, was entirely lost on Rembrandt's contemporaries and aroused none of the enthusiasm that greeted the great works of the masters of the Italian Renaissance when they first appeared. When Rembrandt created his sublimest works, he was a forgotten man, completely out of touch with the tastes and fashions of his time, a disregarded survivor from a bygone age. With the *Denial of St Peter* Rembrandt reinstated the old Caravaggesque composition of half-length figure groups with artificial light effects. In doing so he came back to his point of departure, as if to say: Even those

*The Denial of St Peter, 1660. Rijksmuseum, Amsterdam.*

poor followers of the Italians at Utrecht and Amsterdam had a larger share in the heritage of a great age than have the artists of the present day. As a result of his reversion to Caravaggesque composition, however, his paintings served as a sharp criticism of the old Dutch Italianists of his youth. He revitalized their hackneyed formulas with that life-giving breath of the spirit over which they had no command. In the group before the open hearth of the guard room he conjures up a whole archaic past. Rough soldiers fill the foreground, their huge figures cut short by the picture frame. A sturdy centurion sits in an armchair, over which he has thrown his leather-red coat; lifting a bulky calabash to his thirsty lips, he pauses and glances mistrustfully at the Apostle. An unseen fire casts glowing reflections on his somber body-armor. The middle group is placed in the fullest light, the spiritualized face of St Peter contrasting with the barbaric uncouthness of the centurion's. Peter conforms to the "Homer" type as conceived and standardized by Rembrandt himself, the pagan and the Christian ideal man blended in a profoundly human personality. His white garments are flooded with light from the candle held up to his face by the maid-servant, whose form becomes translucent, glowing with a delicate pink radiance. St Peter's figure, largely modeled with the palette knife, has all the firmness and clarity of a piece of classical sculpture, yet it is as tremulous and airy as a cloud. In the faint light of the background, to the right, a group of standing figures is sketched in with lambent strokes of the brush. One of them turns, looking back: the Lord. No more than the faint suggestion of a reproachful glance, but enough to signify the breach of trust and love: "and immediately the cock crew."

As early as the 1630s Rembrandt had aspired to undertake large-scale works. The commission for the *Night Watch* enabled him to prove his genius for monumental painting, but in doing so he alienated his public. Finally, in his old age, came an opportunity for a monumental painting on the grand scale. The new City Hall, memorial to the civic pride of seventeenth-century Amsterdam, was nearing completion. To decorate the main gallery, a number of prominent artists were asked

*The Conspiracy of Julius Civilis, 1661. Nationalmuseum, Stockholm.*

to contribute gigantic mural paintings illustrating different episodes in the story of the Dutch national hero, Julius Civilis, leader of the Batavian revolt against the Romans in 69 A.D. To Rembrandt was allotted a banquet scene with the Batavian conspirators pledging oath by night in the "sacred grove." On this theme he created what must have been his greatest work, not only as regards mere size but also for its artistic import. The history of this picture is a tragic one and strikingly illustrates the gulf that now separated Rembrandt from his contemporaries.

A preliminary sketch in the Graphische Sammlung at Munich, made in 1661, shows what the completed painting looked like. The conspirators are gathered in a vaulted hall with open archways. In the center, on a platform above a broad flight of steps, flanked by stone lions in the style of Hittite sculpture, stands the banquet table with the assembled Batavians. A curtain screens the gathering off from the outside world. Reflections from the brightly lit table dance on the vaults above. In this, its original form, the picture must have produced an almost overwhelming impression of grandeur and majesty.

Such was the state of the painting when it was delivered by the artist and hung in its appointed place early in 1662. But the municipal authorities were not satisfied and the work was returned to Rembrandt for modifications. In such cases the master invariably showed himself unco-operative, if not intractable. By the end of the year he had failed to make any change in the picture, so the vacant wall-space was filled with an indifferent canvas hastily executed by Juriaen Ovens. Rembrandt's masterpiece was never restored to its rightful place. Left with the huge, unutilizable canvas on his hands, Rembrandt decided to perform a drastic operation. He cut away everything but the central group of conspirators around the table and refashioned this fragment to a unified whole. Basing that unity on the table, he extended it across the entire length of the picture, which he transformed into a Caravaggesque candlelight scene, adding to the foreground a new figure, seen from behind, which looms out of bottomless depths of darkness.

Working over this mere fragment of the original painting, he welded it into a dense and flawless whole, and for all its mighty grandeur gave it an aspect of luminous, mysterious lightness. For the last time he summoned up memories of Leonardo's *Last Supper*, which had so much impressed him in his youth. A one-eyed colossus crossing swords with his fellow conspirators, Julius Civilis towers above them all. On his head is a tiara whose form Rembrandt copied from a medal by Pisanello. Gestures and movements are ponderous and clumsy, like those of peasants or members of some primitive tribe, but full of

*Monk Reading, 1661. Atheneum, Helsinki.*

indomitable will-power and resolve. Medieval and Renaissance elements are freely intermingled—Rembrandt aimed at evoking the elemental, age-old instincts of a primitive culture. Though lit up from below their faces seem like eerie masks, such is their intensity of expression that they have an almost hallucinating effect. Colors are opalescent in the candlelight, dappled with warm reflections in the shadows, and all substance becomes incorporeal.

Most of Rembrandt's works of the 1660s deal with a single isolated figure. Unknown in Protestant Holland were the pictures of saints that abounded in Catholic countries, where El Greco, Feti, Rubens and Van Dyck produced great cycles of devotional paintings representing Christ, the Virgin and the Apostles, idealized embodiments of noble religious and ethical qualities rather than portrayals of individual men and women. Strangely enough, the Protestant Rembrandt turned to these themes at the end of his life, and must have done so on his own initiative for no parish in Holland was likely to order such works. As he grew older he turned more and more to portrayals of solitary figures profoundly wrapped in thought. Among his models we find Jews and Christians, Dutchmen and Slavic types that might be Russian pilgrims, but always real people whose features bear the stamp of many sorrows and the buffetings of fate. He painted these people as independent portrait studies, but sometimes gave them a religious significance, building them up into portrayals of Christ and His disciples. Thus in these likenesses he brought the sacred and the profane so close to each other that they tended to coalesce. By 1657 he had already begun a picture cycle of this kind, but soon discontinued it. In 1660-1661, years that saw some of his greatest achievements as a painter, he reverted to this order of ideas and embodied them in a whole series of powerfully handled, deeply moving works. Wearing a monk's cowl and a serene expression of inner peace, his son Titus is portrayed as St Francis (Amsterdam). Then there is the *Monk Reading* (Helsinki); the *Man Praying* (Cleveland); *The Nun* (Epinal), who has the aspect of the grief-stricken Virgin at the foot of the Cross. Once again he undertook a cycle of Apostles: extant are *St Simon* (Kunsthaus, Zurich), *St Bartholomew* (Paul Getty Collection), *St James the Greater* (Metropolitan Museum, New York), *St Paul* (Rijksmuseum, Amsterdam) and *St Matthew* (Louvre). The cycle concludes with *Christ with a Pilgrim's Staff* (Metropolitan Museum, New York), a figure strangely hieratic as a Byzantine icon. Even the Evangelists seem to have been included in this cycle, for we can tentatively identify St John in a picture in Boston Museum and St Luke in the portrait of a man in medieval costume in the Boymans-van Beuningen Museum, Rotterdam.

*St Matthew and the Angel, 1661. Musée du Louvre, Paris.*

Rembrandt's Apostles are not ideal types, but figures from real life. They are rough men, poor and unpretentious; once they were hardened skeptics, like all men on the dark side of life, but they are firm believers now that their eyes have been opened by the miracle that has befallen them. St Matthew is the clearest illustration of the call that came to each of these holy men, the inner summons they heard and obeyed. He breaks off his writing and listens. The voice of the Lord, which called the publican from his toll-collecting, sounds once more in his consciousness, bidding him to his lofty mission. He does not see the angel (whose features are those of Titus) behind him, who lightly brushes against his shoulder and whispers in his ear. Stricken with wonder, the Apostle lifts a wrinkled hand to his breast, as if the voice were ringing in his heart. Matthew is a pictorial equivalent of the following words: "The pious student of Christ's teaching must finally realize that of all things needful the most needful is God. This involves a further consequence. Once he has realized the necessity of turning from outward things into himself, then he will recognize that the *one thing needful* is to turn back from oneself to one's primal origin, which is God."

The man who wrote these words was perhaps the most sensible, the most human, the most Christian-minded thinker of Rembrandt's time: Comenius. Though late in life both men lived fairly close to each other in the same parish, there is no evidence to show that they ever met. The fact remains, however, that we find between them that deep-seated communion of thought and feeling which often unites great minds living in the same age, even when there is no direct contact between them. It has been rightly said of Rembrandt's pictures of saints that their Christianity is neither Protestant nor Catholic, but simply Christian, like that of the Primitive Christians. The same may be said of Comenius' Christianity. The last paintings of Rembrandt, like the last writings of Comenius, are direct and human in their appeal. Both were great teachers, great educators of humanity. Rembrandt portrayed himself as St Paul in the cycle of Apostles, as one who "out of

*The Syndics of the Drapers' Guild, 1662. Rijksmuseum, Amsterdam.*

the labyrinth of the world has found his way to the paradise of the heart." His face is tranfigured by the tenderest, most visionary penumbra that Rembrandt ever poured into a picture. In his youth he had often included himself among those taking part in the episodes of the Passion. But this is the exalted climax of his self-identification with the great figures of the dawn of Christianity: Rembrandt himself comes toward us in the person of one of those greatly privileged men who walked the earth in the days of Our Lord. He opens the Book of Scriptures and looks at us with questioning eyes. He seems to be weighing in the balance many things on which men set great store: success, wealth, honors, everything that men associate with a happy life. He knows the vanity of it all; he had held it in his hands and it ran through his fingers like sand. What remains is but the one thing needful. "For the Bible is a book of the greatest necessity, such as no other under the sun, if a man is to avoid the path to eternal perdition and regain salvation" (*Unum necessarium*).

Although in his old age Rembrandt executed his portrait commissions in a manner that fully answered to his own artistic aspirations, he must have succeeded in satisfying his models at the same time, for he received more and more orders for portraits toward the end of his life. His interpretations not only plumbed the depths of the human heart, but were true to character in the highest degree; his sitters were forced to recognize a faithful likeness. Thus it was that he received an order for what was to be his most significant group portrait, that of the "Staalmeesters" or *Syndics of the Drapers' Guild* (1662, Amsterdam).

Rembrandt's portrayal of the human figure was now so universal in its implications that he could approach the theme quite objectively and be true to life, refraining from the arbitrary transformations he had imposed on the *Night Watch*. The board of syndics is conferring in the guild hall around a table spread with an oriental carpet of vivid red, patterned with designs in golden yellow. The board members stand out behind it in their solemn suits of black with bluish-white collars. The viewpoint of the spectator is lower than the table-top and this heightens the effect that Rembrandt aimed at, of bringing all elements on to the picture surface. Seated in the center, the chairman is quietly, but with the speaking gesture of an experienced orator, commenting on a point in the statute book that has just been under discussion. His exposé is coming to a close, the meeting is about to be adjourned; one man has risen to his feet, a second has pushed back his chair, a third is picking up his gloves. At this moment the visitor enters the room, causing a slight diversion; four members glance toward him; only the chairman, still engrossed in his subject, pays no heed. X-ray examination has

*Laughing Self-Portrait, ca. 1663. Wallraf-Richartz Museum, Cologne.*

revealed a great many pentimenti in the painting, which goes to show how long Rembrandt worked over it until he got the effect he wanted (the servant at the back, for example, changed position three times). Concealed behind its air of simplicity are the knowledge and experience of a lifetime, which enabled the painter to lighten and relax the taut symmetry and uniformity of the composition with such wonderful skill. The result is consummate spiritual and pictorial unity;

*The Jewish Bride (detail), 1665. Rijksmuseum, Amsterdam.*

the picture is, at one and the same time, an exemplary realization of the traditional Dutch conception of this theme and the definitive fulfillment of Rembrandt's personal, long-standing quest of inner unity. With this work Dutch portrait painting reached its highest point.

The exact dates of Rembrandt's last works are wanting, and as there are very few preliminary drawings to guide us, attempts at dating are necessarily vague. Rembrandt's impasto had now become so thick that Houbraken was moved to write that "you could take a Rembrandt portrait by the nose!" Not until two centuries later, with Monticelli, the early Cézanne and Van Gogh, did any painter again venture to lay in such masses of pigment on the canvas. Sometimes the result is not unlike that of the volcano-pitted landscapes in the etchings of Hercules Seghers, or the crust of some dead planet. Backgrounds are saturated with a heavy umber, the hue of mineral pitch, against which figures stand out with a smoldering brilliance of uncanny intensity. Such is the textural quality of the *Laughing Self-Portrait* in Cologne with its bold gamut of reds in the wrinkled face and golds in the clothes. Possibly this is an allusion to Heraclitus, the laughing philosopher, who with Democritus, his weeping counterpart, was a favorite theme with the Caravaggeschi, but the incorporation in a self-portrait produces an effect of startling directness. Rembrandt is laughing as he did in many a grimacing self-portrait of youthful days, but an abyss of experience and disillusionment lies between those laughters. Here we have the silent inner laugh of an old man who has been thrust aside by the jostling crowd, who has seen through all the vanity of life—a laugh full of tragic grandeur. ("But what will the admirers of human wisdom say to that? They will surely scoff at the old fool who from the peak of honor comes down to the lowest depths of humiliation. Let them laugh, if such is their pleasure. My heart too laughs, for joy at having escaped the paths of error. I have found the haven, farewell to fate and fortune!" – Comenius, *Unum necessarium*, chapter X).

For all its richness and splendor, the *matière* of painting is never an end in itself with Rembrandt, but a means of embodying his innermost thoughts. Such is the case with the *Jewish Bride* (Amsterdam). After countless attempts to explain this picture, its exact meaning remains a riddle. The magnificent, old-world garments worn by the couple are oriental in character. Isaac and Rebecca, Jacob and Rachel, Tobias and Sarah have all been suggested as the theme. Perhaps it is simply a double portrait; Schmidt-Degener tentatively identified the husband with the man portrayed in a small single portrait in the Bache Collection. Yet

*The Jewish Bride, 1665. Rijksmuseum, Amsterdam.*

the posing of the figures in their glittering garments of scarlet and gold against the dim background of an abandoned park, and the ritual gesture of the man, laying his hand on his wife's breast, seem to point to the fulfillment of a biblical destiny. The human element of such a portrait is so deep and universal in significance that living models, contemporaries of the artist, are turned into the timeless heroes of the

Old Testament and symbolize eternal spiritual values. The colors are an integrating part of the mystical symbolism.

Also dating from the very end of Rembrandt's life is the Brunswick *Family Portrait*. This has been regarded as an unfinished work but, as it is signed, Rembrandt must have felt that he had said all he had to say and left it deliberately in its present state. According to Hou-

*Family Portrait, ca. 1668. Herzog Anton Ulrich Museum, Brunswick.*

*The Return of the Prodigal Son, 1668. Hermitage, Leningrad.*

braken, Rembrandt justified his methods with the words: "A picture is finished when the artist has fulfilled his purpose in undertaking it." The spiritual radiation of the colors is such that they seem aflame, particularly in the figures of the mother and baby daughter. Apparently he brushed in the faces and then modeled them directly with his finger; the rest he built up chiefly with the palette knife. The very dark ground color is a blackened gold-brown that everywhere shows through since there are no evenly brushed layers of pigment as in earlier works. The mother is dressed in glowing brick-red, the child on her knee in

*Simeon in the Temple, ca. 1669. Nationalmuseum, Stockholm.*

iridescent salmon-pink; the older girl on the far left is a silvery olive-grey, the other a luminous blue-green. The red, green and yellow flowers in the basket shine like jewels; or better, scintillate like electric sparks. Against the dark ground the figures stand out like radiant flowers amid an unearthly glitter of colors. The little girl seems like a creature fading away into the Other World. The father's somber form casts a suggestion of protective warmth over these spectral colors; it completes the solid, unobtrusive trapezoid of the pictorial architecture.

The art of painting could go no further. Explanation and analysis can serve no purpose now, and at this point words fail the art historian. Only a poet in whom some spark of Rembrandt's fire lives on could hope to describe this picture adequately.

The limit of the painter's physical medium is reached not only in the *Family Portrait* but also in the *Return of the Prodigal Son* in the Hermitage. Physical substance is now no more than the outward manifestation of an ultimate spiritual essence. With infinite love, like an image of the Heavenly Father, the old man embraces the kneeling penitent and draws him to his bosom. The onlookers fade into the darkness and all we see is the essential. The prodigal's face is turned away, but we are made aware of the powerful uprush of tears that convulses his whole being. His tattered clothing flares in the light like the costliest attire, for it is the garb of his humility.

When Rembrandt died in 1669, he left an unfinished painting on the easel in his studio: *Simeon in the Temple*, showing the old man praying to God to let His servant go in peace now that he has seen the Light of the World. There the painter Allaert van Everdingen saw the picture soon after the master's death. It has been identified with that noble ruin of a picture now in the National Museum in Stockholm; even in its greatly damaged state it affords a moving testimony of Rembrandt's art at the end of his life. Simeon's transfigured hands bear the inimitable mark of Rembrandt's brush. This picture might be an illustration of the words of Comenius: "Death is the last line written by life. So that if the end be good, then all is well."

# LIST OF ILLUSTRATIONS

*(Unless otherwise specified, all illustrations are from archive photographs.)*

PRINTED BY
IRL IMPRIMERIES RÉUNIES LAUSANNE S.A.

BOUND BY
MAYER ET SOUTTER S.A., RENENS-LAUSANNE

Printed in Switzerland